Maximum Insecurity

A Doctor in the Supermax

WILLIAM WRIGHT, M.D.

The people and events in this book are real. Since the characters sometimes lack a sense of humor, I've changed many of the names.

ISBN: 1492895202
ISBN 13: 9781492895206
Library of Congress Control Number: 2013919324
CreateSpace Independent Publishing Platform
North Charleston, South Carolina

Dedication

To Mollie and the Fur People

TABLE OF CONTENTS

INTRODUCTION

Colorado State Penitentiary squats like a brown toad on a sunblasted plain of stunted piñon and sagebrush, literally the end of the road. I hesitated before pressing the steel button of the main gate squawk box, hearing the raucous multilingual shouts from the housing pods even out in the parking lot. I clutched at my only weapon—a stethoscope. *What the hell was I doing here?*

This is the story of my odyssey from a comfortable career as a Midwestern ear surgeon to life as the sole physician for Colorado's maximum security prison. It is an eyewitness account of practicing medicine among the state's most violent and predatory criminals. I was not a visiting journalist with a notepad getting the spruced-up VIP tour. This was where I was to live and work.

After thirty-plus years as an ear doctor, I was bored. Burned out. I'd seen it all, done it all, got the T-shirt, etc. I needed to do something different. I saw an ad from the Colorado Department of Corrections (CDOC) looking for doctors. This was different. It sounded intriguing, exotic with a hint of danger. I applied.

They were looking for general medical doctors. I was a neuro-otologist, a fancy name for a cross between an ear doctor and a neurosurgeon. If the medical mainstream orbits the sun, I was on Pluto. Desperation prevailed. They hired me.

My wife, much more sensible than I, balked at my announcement of a career change. She's a very diplomatic woman, but the essence of her response was: *Are you crazy!* I had no good response to that. She was probably right, but I stuck to my decision to change. I let go of the trapeze and soared toward the world of correctional medicine.

Now that I had the job, I wondered if I could pull it off. I dimly remembered life as a general physician before I became a specialist. Sure. I could do this. I used to be a real doctor. The excitement and glamour of being a prison doctor beckoned.

What is the attraction of such institutions that draws us by the millions to watch reality shows about prisons and medical dramas? For the vast majority of us, the criminal justice system is something we'll never personally experience. Ending up in a supermax prison is even less likely.

Likewise, intimate acquaintance with the workings of medicine is usually something people try to avoid. It's all too alien and scary. Still, from a safe distance, we're naturally curious about these other worlds.

Prisons fascinate us. Mystery, danger, violence, crime, life and death—all the things that make life worthwhile. Medicine is intriguing too. Doctors are modern high priests, working their miracles behind drapes of secrecy. Physicians have the mystery, life and death stuff down even if we come up short on crime and violence. Still, people watch crime, prison and medical shows on TV by the dozen, so it seemed a likely subject for a book when I became the doctor at Colorado's supermax prison.

For those of you with the same fascinations, this is an opportunity to peek over the prison walls and into the life of a physician dealing with the most heinous people our society produces.

ONE

THE BOMB

"Are you out of your mind?" My wife, Mollie, set aside the half-dried dish, threw the towel into the sink and whirled on me. "A prison? What do you know about prisons? You're an ear doctor."

"True," I said, backing up a step, "but I'm a burned-out ear doctor. I can't do it anymore. I'm just slogging through the day on a chain gang." I belatedly realized that I'd chosen the wrong metaphor.

My kids already knew I was nuts, but they were grown with families of their own. They didn't get a vote. Mollie, on the other hand, held fifty-one percent of the stock in our marriage. I had to convince the boss.

"I just want to do something different. Maybe just for a little while. A few months. Consider it my midlife crisis."

"I do."

I extracted the handcuffs from my back pocket and held them out, jingling. "Could be fun."

"Oh, please." she said, doing a 180 and grabbing the towel. Mollie spent the next few minutes polishing the same dish. I knew when to shut up.

She finally turned, wiping her hands. "You really want to do this?"

"Yeah, I really do."

"Just for a little while?"

"We'll see how it goes."

That was six years ago.

———

A week in the training academy started my career as the newest doctor in Colorado's maximum-security system. Located on the grounds of a Benedictine monastery in Cañon City, the academy drilled me in protocol, time sheets, proper dress, and where to park.

I also learned that with no provocation whatsoever and at the slightest opportunity, any and all of these offenders would be pleased to slit my throat, rape me, or turn me into a drug mule. Weapons? These guys don't need any stinking weapons. They can disembowel you with a paper clip.

Oh, come on now, I thought. *Who were they trying to scare?* They showed pictures. I was scared. I didn't remember this being mentioned in any of the CDOC promotional literature.

The instructors provided reassuring statistics. The chance of being assaulted in a U.S. prison was only four times as likely as it was walking across the Walmart parking lot. *That wasn't too bad, was it?*

Not to worry, I thought, *the guards would keep the bad guys at bay.* Unfortunately, we had no guards. What we had were "correctional officers" or "COs," and I found out I was one. Unwittingly, I had become a cop by accepting a job in the prison system. I was considered a law enforcement officer, and I'd damn well better behave like one. I wondered whether this could get me out of a parking ticket, but thought it might be gauche to ask. Nobody suggested that I carry a gun.

As a matter of fact, nobody carried guns. What about all those TV shows with the steely-eyed sharpshooters prowling the catwalks waiting for someone to make a false move? Not here. CSP, which holds its inhabitants at the highest level of security, doesn't even have watchtowers. It looks more like an office building that had a budget shortfall when it came to installing the windows.

Next, the instructors informed us that the prison system had no inmates. Previously, they housed prisoners, cons or convicts, then inmates, but now held "offenders." This didn't seem like much of an improvement on the dignity scale.

Like joining any large bureaucracy, I learned the mission statement. This consisted of several paragraphs that said, "Treat the bad guys nice." Immediately following came indoctrination on how to avoid getting scammed, seduced, bullied, or killed in the process.

We learned Pressure Point Control Tactics, PPCT, the "defensive control" techniques designed to immobilize an assailant by attacking specific nerve points. The idea was to take down the attacker without really injuring him.

This is a good system when you're faced with daily lawsuits from offenders who would take a hangnail to the Supreme Court. However, PPCT takes a lot of practice to be effective. I had to master the techniques in a four-hour time window on the monastery front lawn.

I felt pretty confident since I'd studied martial arts for fifteen years. It started out as a post-divorce guy thing, needing to dig myself out of a psychological hole with some physical activity. I'd grown up seeing Charles Atlas ads in magazines and figured that learning how to kick sand in a bully's face might endear me to future females. I found that I really enjoyed it and went on to three black belts and two instructor certificates in tae kwon do and aikido. Now I was poised to add PPCT to the list.

One of the instructors asked me to demonstrate a PPCT strike. I did.

"No, no," he said. "You can't do it that way. You'll hurt the offender."

"Isn't that the point?" I asked.

"Not at all. You want just enough force to neutralize the attack."

"Well, yeah," I said. "But if a crazed 250-pound murderer with a shiv is charging me, I'm not going to get all touchy-feely about putting him down."

"There are cameras everywhere," he said, as if that settled things.

"So?"

"So you'll end up in court on a charge of using excessive force."

"I'll take the chance," I countered. "Otherwise I might end up in the morgue on a charge of using insufficient force."

"Just show me the correct technique."

I shrugged and gave him the PPCT-approved strike that would probably hurt me more than the attacker. "Much better," he said. Class over.

Finally, the time we'd all been waiting for: payroll instruction and fringe benefits. How hard could this be? Harder than you'd imagine unless you already work for the government.

The administrator assigned everyone an employee ID number, thus establishing a kind of numerical parity with the inmates. Then it was time to sign up for the medical plan, dental plan, eye care plan, 401(k) plan. I'd never felt so cared for. I trooped over to Marge, one of the secretaries assigned to welcome us into the bureaucracy. Her tangled bouffant matched her harried features.

Piles of handwritten forms obscured Marge's table. It looked like she used a leaf blower as a desk organizer. She blew a few stray hairs away from her face, barely making eye contact with me. "So what's your ID number?" she growled.

"I'm sorry. I forgot it already. One four something. Can you look it up?"

The exasperation crept into her cigarette voice. "I don't have that list, Just look on the back of your ID card."

"I don't have an ID card yet. They said to come here first."

Marge finally fixed me with a glare that could only have come from being a homicide detective for twenty years. "Right. You sign up for the plans then you get your picture taken for the ID card." She thankfully left out the last part, *"asshole."*

"Can I go get my ID card and then come back?"

Marge rolled her hazel eyes and yelled across the room, "Stan! This guy doesn't remember his ID number." Her tone indicated her opinion about my fitness for duty at CDOC.

Stan, with his own pile of papers, yelled back, "Tell him to look on the back of his ID card."

"He doesn't *have* an ID card."

Stan, stating the obvious, replied, "He's got to have an ID card. He can't get in without one."

"Jesus, Stan, I know that. He needs to *get* one."

"Never mind. I'll make him one. What's his ID number?"

You get the idea. I staggered out of the signup feeling like I'd need one of those plans sooner than I thought.

TWO

FIRST DAY ON THE JOB

I slapped the blaring alarm at five a.m. I used to have a clock with a smiling face and eyes that rolled back and forth. It would chime gently and croon, "Time to start your happy day." I wished to hell I had that clock back.

Showered, shaved, and out the door I plunged into the darkness to make the hour commute to work. I passed the hamlet of Florence, home to the federal supermax prison. Through the pre-dawn gloom, perpetual mercury lights shone down on Ted Kaczynski, Terry Nichols, and a gaggle of Mafiosi and foreign terrorists. If you saw them on the national news, they're in Florence.

Five miles farther west sprawls the 5,000-acre East Cañon Complex. CSP, one of six prisons in the complex, squats well back from the south side of the highway, its chameleon brown shell camouflaged by the barren landscape.

No highway sign announces the presence of CSP. Indeed, the entire complex is totally anonymous. Most people whiz by into the gentle downhill curve toward Cañon City without ever registering that they have just passed the biggest concentration of prisons on the planet.

Cañon City, home to sixteen thousand souls, is a leftover from the Pikes Peak Gold Rush in 1858. Its main claim to fame besides the prisons is the Royal Gorge Bridge, a few miles west of Territorial Correctional

Facility. Until the Beipanjiang River Bridge in China surpassed it in 2003 it was the highest bridge in the world, soaring nearly a thousand feet above whitewater rafters on the Arkansas River.

Like most of the uninitiated, I drove right past the prison and had to ask directions at the local Denny's in Cañon City. "Back out the way you came. Top of the hill around the big curve on the right. Can't miss it."

I got it the second time around, pulling up to a guard shack several hundred yards off the highway and fumbling my newly minted credentials toward the officer. He waved me on, repeating the gesture impatiently when I didn't move along. I rolled down the window.

"Which one is CSP?" I asked.

"First on the right. Can't miss it."

A sign up ahead declared this brown toad of a building was indeed the Colorado State Penitentiary. I guess I'd expected guard towers and prowling Dobermans, but this looked more like a huge office building, albeit surrounded by fencing festooned with rolls of razor wire.

I parked my battered '98 Honda outside a chain-link fence and walked to the gate. Two huge flagpoles flying the U.S. and Colorado flags flanked fifty yards of concrete walkway between the gate and twin granite arches marking the prison entrance. Arid wind blew off the Dakota hogbacks west of town, swirling ochre dust devils around the vast asphalt parking lot. Nothing else stirred. Was I in the right place? I pronounced my name to the faceless squawk box below a surveillance camera.

"Who?" came the tinny reply.

"Dr. Wright. I'm the new doctor."

"Just a minute."

When you think of the entrance to a maximum security prison, ominous images arise. So what did I see looking through the chain-link toward the hulking entrance?

Bunnies. The immaculate green lawn was alive with dozens of cotton-tailed bunnies. The more I looked, the more appeared. Under bushes. In the well-tended mini-gardens by the gate. Hopping across the grass. Elysium.

The gate clanked open. "Sorry, Doc," said the box. "Had to check."

The walk from the gate to the entry had its own touch of unreality. Besides taking care not to step on the rabbits, I felt on display to the hundreds of slit-like windows fronting the building. Some were cell windows, while others opened from the tiny recreation rooms called day halls.

Each inmate occupied his solitary cell twenty-three hours a day. Ten minutes of the remaining hour was spent taking a shower in a telephone booth-sized room with fifty minutes of "recreation" time left over to spend alone in a bare room only slightly larger than his cell, furnished with just a chin-up bar. The day hall windows, about six inches wide and four feet tall, were open to the outside. Most were occupied by offenders yelling conversations in Spanish or English to other windows.

All of the inmates must have gotten copies of my employment application and working schedule. I wasn't ten feet past the gate when cries rang out: "Hey, Doc, welcome to CSP!" "My back hurts!" "You get me something for my bowels, eh?" My shoulders hunched. I felt like a bug under a magnifying glass.

Later, I learned the day hall windows also served as major avenues for passing contraband back and forth from one level to another. The offender on one level brings a contraband item to the day hall and connects it to a ratline. A ratline consists of a long string made out of anything flexible; pieces of bedding, underwear, rolled toilet paper, and a lot of other things too gross to contemplate.

With a small weight attached to the end, the ratline whips across the floor to another cell or drops through the window to the next level. Adroitness born of endless practice, inmates pendulum items to adjacent windows or even to the level above.

Finally out of sight of the day hall windows, I reached the prison proper through two sets of heavy double doors. The main lobby was spacious and fluorescently institutional. My first human being, a uniformed CO, stood behind a broad entry station. He checked my ID card, searched my lunch bag and waved me through the metal detector.

"Hey, Doc," he called as I turned away. I cringed involuntarily. Busted already.

He pointed to the time clock. "Don't forget to punch in."

Nodding, I swiped my card. My name glowed on the LCD screen. I was officially in prison.

Ahead, a battleship gray door rattled on an overhead rack-and-pinion gear and crashed open, revealing a small room leading into the prison depths. It was closed off by another door at its far end. This entrance, called a sally port, is a box with a remotely operated door on either end and claustrophobia in the middle. It marks the last glimpse of normal life anyone would see on entering CSP. I glanced up, half-expecting to see Dante's "All Hope Abandon Ye Who Enter Here" inscribed above the portal.

Instead, a stocky woman in scrubs bounced out of the sally port, hand extended. "You must be Dr. Wright," she gushed, "Welcome to CSP." Heavy-framed glasses rode above a perpetual smile, daring the world to try to ruffle her feathers.

She tapped her nametag. "I'm Sabrina, the head nurse." Sabrina, I learned, was the sergeant-at-arms of the nursing staff. She swept toward the maw of the port. "Come on. I'll give you the grand tour."

CSP is a formidable place to enter. Like an airlock, the two doors of a sally port are never open at the same time. The bulletproof glass in the opposite door winked at me. "Come on, Kid," it said. "Just step into the little box. Come on..."

Was it too late to bolt for the entry across the lobby? *This is stupid,* I told myself. *Nothing to worry about. It's only a maximum-security prison filled with murderers.*

Sabrina must have sensed her quarry was about to make a run for it. As only a nurse or a mother can do, she gently, but firmly, gripped my elbow and urged me forward into the port. Flashback. It's time for your bath, young man. March! I marched.

The door, unbidden, clanked closed behind us and pounded shut with a finality that brought back all the images and dread of an Edgar Allen Poe tale. I felt like I'd been shrink-wrapped.

The main prison sally port sported bulletproof glass above waist level on the sidewalls. A revolving bin like a bank's night depository embedded into the cinder block wall beneath the glass allowed items to pass back and forth to the control room beyond.

"Here's where you get your keys," Sabrina said. "Just give them your chit and they'll return the keys in the same slot. Don't forget to sign the log."

"Chit?" I said.

Sabrina held up a metal tag with her name engraved in block letters. "Chit," she said by way of explanation. "This way they know who's got the keys."

"Always good to know," I agreed.

Chits and keys clanged back and forth. Sabrina said a cheery "Hi" to a figure in the darkened master control center behind the glass. Why did they keep it so dark? What were they hiding? The only thing missing were red eyes glowing in the corners.

Master control consisted of an area big enough to parallel park three Volkswagen buses. Running alongside the sally port like a house trailer, one end of the master control protruded back into the lobby and the other into the main hall of the prison beyond the sally port. I could faintly see pegboards of keys, radios, and unrecognizable lumps of equipment. Computer screens seemed to provide the only illumination with views of various doors, corridors, and distant rooms displayed.

I glimpsed a dim figure working a trackball on a computer. The inner door of the sally port rumbled back, but I stood rooted to the spot. I looked back over my shoulder and started to turn. "I think I'll just…"

"This way," Sabrina chirped, executing a perfect PPCT grip on my elbow.

I am not claustrophobic. I've crawled through caves where I didn't have enough room to turn my head. *I could do this. No problem.* Still, I felt such a sense of dread and crushing isolation staring at that opening, my feet refused to move.

Sabrina's hand applied a little more pressure, and I was propelled forward. She had apparently paid closer attention to the PPCT class than I had.

Her arm swept across a wide, well-lit corridor with branches running off in three directions. "This is the main hall," Sabrina said, apparently trying to distract me from the slider sealing behind us.

I'd like to say that I handled it with aplomb, but I didn't. I clutched. A true sense of panic welled up and I felt like I was going to totally lose it, scrabbling at the port door, pounding and begging for escape.

Sabrina had seen this deer-in-the-headlights phenomenon before. She centered herself before my contracting field of vision and gave me her best hundred-watt smile. "Not what you expected?"

"Not exactly," I croaked, swallowing hard and trying to get my breath going again.

"You'll get used to it." That sounded like a threat. She nudged me to the left. "Let's see one of the housing pods. Stand here so they can see you."

"Who?"

"The control center. See the camera through the window?"

Searching the ceiling, I saw a security camera with its monocular eye directed impassively toward the window.

"If you stand off to the side they might not see you," she said patiently. "Or they might think you didn't want to go through this door."

"How do they know we're here?"

"They're always watching the cameras. When they see someone standing in front of a door, they open it and let you pass. At least if they recognize you. If they don't, they might ask for your name and ID over the speaker." She indicated a metal grill inset with a large button in the side wall.

"And the button?"

"That gets their attention if necessary. But don't use it. It irritates them if they're busy with something else. Just wait. It might take a minute."

I wanted to be sure I had this straight. "So the button is a call button that we don't use to call anyone."

"Right."

With a metallic *thunk*, the door cranked open. I kind of expected these massive doors to slide smoothly like the bridge on *Star Trek*. Not these guys. They clanked and shuddered in their tracks like an underground tomb in an Indiana Jones movie. The slab rammed home behind us with finality. *Gotcha, Kid!*

I squinted through the glass panel forming the far end of the sally port, seeing nothing but empty corridor ahead. I peered over my shoulder. Emptiness behind. I thought prisons were busy places. Where was everybody? I was looking at another call button that I knew I wasn't supposed to use. What if they weren't paying attention? What if they didn't let me out? In a sally port, can they hear you scream?

A-Pod was constructed as an octagon with a tube sticking out one side. We were in the tube part, which connected to the main prison core behind us.

The walls of the connecting tube were barren concrete block save for a single glass-walled room on either side of the corridor. Each was the size of a large walk-in closet. One contained a medical examination table, the other a barber's chair. "The pod's medical exam room," Sabrina said, indicating the former. My domain.

"So this is where I see everybody?"

"Well, you can, but the big exam room and your office with the computer is downstairs. This is really more for quick and dirty stuff if you happen to be up on the pod."

As we approached the interior of the pod the ceiling rose to two stories. An office for the COs formed the first floor of the central hub, the darkened control area stacked on top. Eight wedge-shaped housing units radiated out like sections of an orange, separated from the hub by a wall of bulletproof Lexan.

Each unit contained eight cells on each of two levels, all visible from the central control area. No bars here. The cells boasted solid steel doors with a thin vertical window and a tray slot facing the interior of the pod. Each level also had a telephone booth-sized shower room and a Lexan-faced day hall or exercise room.

No big screen TV and lounge chair for this day hall. The area, only slightly bigger than a regular eight-by-ten cell, was bare except for a chin-up bar bolted to an inner wall. I could see a solitary man exercising on each tier. Some did calisthenics or used the chin-up bar. Some looked out the narrow windows, open to the outside where catcalls had pelted me when I walked in from the outer gate. Some just paced the perimeter of the small room like caged animals.

Three tall thin rectangles of light marked the far wall of each sixteen-cell housing unit where the high desert light of Colorado streamed onto the smooth expanse of grey concrete floor. The stark concrete was interrupted only by a telephone bolted to one wall with yellow tape outlining a rectangle on the floor where the caller was permitted to stand. During calls, the inmate was handcuffed to a steel D-ring embedded in the wall, preventing him from wandering off during the conversation.

Sabrina strode around the control center and paused outside the door to the empty office. "Hi, Krause," she said.

Determined not to appear even greener by asking where Krause might be hiding in this glass-walled space, I glanced furtively into the office, peering under the table occupying the center of the room and trying to examine it for hidden corners. "Yo, Sabrina," came the answer from above.

A short overhead passage connected a stairwell in the outside wall of the housing unit to the control area of the polygonal control tower. A steel grate with a hinged hatch formed part of the floor of the passage. Krause straddled the grate, prepared to lower a bucket on a rope. "Need a key?" he offered.

"Key?" I said. "I thought everything was electronic."

"For the tray slots," Sabrina explained. "We pass medications through the slots. The control officer passes us the key in the bucket if we need it."

She craned her neck upward. "Nope. Just taking Doc on a tour."

I waved upward at Krause's crotch. "Nice to meet you."

"You too, Doc."

Everybody automatically knew my name. I was "Doc", like one of the dwarves. On the other hand, I would have to identify my co-workers by their tread patterns.

We continued our circle of the corridor surrounding the control center. Looking outward I could see uniformed figures climbing the steel staircases to the upper tiers and escorting inmates to and from the showers and day halls as we passed each housing unit section. Two officers always accompanied each offender and no two offenders were ever out of their cells at the same time.

Despite the bright florescent lighting and large open spaces, the whole atmosphere was oppressive with an undercurrent of barely contained horror, depression and desperation. The pods echoed with callisthenic cadences, complaints shouted at COs, or just unintelligible howls.

"Let's see Medical," Sabrina said. My elbow was already sore, so I readily agreed.

We descended two stories in a cinderblock stairwell deep underground to another locked door. Poe again. *The Cask of Amontillado.* Sabrina pushed the button on the wall.

"I thought you weren't supposed to call them," I said, gesturing toward the button.

The door clicked. "This doesn't call anyone," she said. "You just push the button to open the door."

"So how do you tell the difference?"

Sabrina paused halfway through the door. "Buttons in stairwells open the doors. Buttons on walls in the pods are call buttons." She turned to enter the hallway, but then turned back to me. "But some doors open with your key card and some need a regular key. Some don't need keys at all."

"Right," I said, trying to avoid any more explanation.

Sabrina stepped into the hallway and turned left into a small lobby. "No prisoner cells down here," she said, "except for temporary holding cells in Intake and Medical. Speaking of which..."

Sure enough. A glassed door boasted a plastic sign declaring this the *CSP Medical Clinic.* Home sweet home.

The control center buzzed us in to medical's modest lobby, basically a wide spot in the corridor circling the central hub. Two nurses looked up and gave us a tentative smile reserved for possible sources of trouble or work. I was introduced as the new doctor. Attitudes changed. They were thrilled. Really.

Chronically short-staffed, Centennial, the old supermax prison next door, and Colorado State Penitentiary had no physician of their own. Physicians from other prison facilities came over to put out fires and take care of major health problems. Sabrina informed me that I was now the physician for both. Surprise!

Four nurses prepared medications twice daily and delivered them door-to-door for 750 inmates at CSP. In addition, they drew blood samples, did cardiograms, and ran triage on the hundreds of daily crises their miscreant patients dreamed up.

Without a physician around, the necessity to make significant medical decisions often fell to the nurses. This added a lot of pressure, and they weren't happy about it. With my arrival they had somebody who was all theirs. You could smell the confetti and party hats.

Sabrina led me down the hall to another steel door. *Physician* was carved into a plastic nameplate stuck to the wall.

"Me?" I said.

"You," she nodded.

The door was, of course, locked and the office dark. No wall button visible.

"You need a restricted key for this one," she said. "You'll have to sign it out in master control upstairs."

We continued around the medical unit with introductions to the scheduler, secretary, and finally my immediate boss, Blair, the Health Services Administrator (HSA). Her long blonde hair framed a thin face that had dealt with way too much aggravation.

"Nice to be here," I said.

"You have no idea," she said.

Her office was as spartan as the rest of the medical suite. A few family pictures and a couple of small Walmart art prints stuck on the side of a filing cabinet completed the décor. Like all offices at CSP, Blair's sported a gray-brown steel door, beige cinderblock walls, cement floor, and embedded wire mesh in the hall window. Since the medical suite was in the basement, there wasn't even a tiny window to the outside. Claustrophobia loomed again.

"You're getting the tour?" she said. "What do you think?"

"I think it's going to be a little different from private practice," I managed.

She laughed. "Yes, it's not like practicing medicine on the outside. You'll get used to it. Just remember..." Her phone rang.

"I know," I said, trying to come across as lighthearted. "Everybody is out to kill me."

She picked up the phone, covering the mouthpiece with her hand. "Well, yes. But don't let that bother you. It's really a great place to work. Glad you're on board." She lifted the phone and gave us a little wave. Sabrina nudged me. Time to move on.

We retraced our steps to the lobby, and Sabrina shepherded me to the parking lot. "That's a quick run through. Dr. McIntyre will get you oriented on the day-to-day stuff. He's been here forever and knows all the ropes. He's at Fremont." She smiled hopefully.

"Fremont..."

"You don't know where Fremont is? Well, I guess you wouldn't. After all, there are plenty of prisons out here." She took out a piece of paper and drew a map. "Here we are at CSP. Centennial is just across the main road." She tapped a square on her map. "Next is Arrowhead, then Four Mile, Skyline, and then Fremont. If you go too far a patrol car will run you down and arrest you." I blinked. "Just kidding," she said. "But they will turn you around with a warning. Don't worry, you can't miss Fremont."

THREE

FREMONT

I t turns out I didn't miss it. I tooled down the interior road in excess of the fifteen mph speed limit and quickly acquired a grim-faced security patrol escort.

I flashed my most ingenuous smile. "New guy."

"Right," growled Smokey, not a wrinkle of humor showing behind his Ray-Bans.

"I'm the new doc," I stumbled on. "I'm supposed to go to the Fremont medical clinic."

If he recognized my exalted status, he kept it well hidden. "Follow me," he said. "Slowly."

I was a little put out at the gruffness, but it made sense. A fast-moving car in the interior of a prison complex was a red flag. So was someone walking or running in between the prisons.

Before I arrived, a physician worked here who was a runner. He liked to get a little exercise by running between the various clinics he was staffing in different prisons. After the third time he got busted by the security patrols, his HSA took him aside and explained the facts of life. Walk to your car. Drive to the next prison. Walk inside. No running. Just like at the swimming pool.

Fremont, a medium security Level III prison, was more like what I'd seen on TV. After passing through the front blockhouse metal detector and sally port, I emerged into a spacious lawn with a concrete path lined with flowers. Of course, there were the double chain link fences topped with rolls of razor wire, but compared with the depths of CSP it was downright cheery.

Past a couple more gates I emerged into the main concrete-paved yard. A hoard of offenders returning from chow surrounded me. Whoa!

I was acutely aware of the flood of unshackled murderers, rapists, and jaywalkers. The training academy pictures flashed unbidden before my eyes. My shoulders tensed. Where were the guards? Had I blundered into a restricted area? Would they ever find the body?

Yet nobody paid me the slightest attention. A wave of relief and disappointment crested.

Hundreds of convicted felons ambled by, chatting and joking like they were taking a lap around the park before returning to the office. I spotted a few COs in the yard, without weapons and outnumbered by a couple of orders of magnitude by their charges. All the offenders wore green scrub suits while I, like a whore in church, stood there in my yellow dress shirt and red tie.

One of the men stopped and looked at me curiously. "You lost, Sport?"

Tensed for a confrontation, I ventured, "I'm looking for the medical clinic."

He pointed to a large, hand-lettered sign over a door about ten feet away. *Medical Clinic.* "Try that one," he suggested.

Inside, it looked like a real medical clinic, albeit one in a bad neighborhood. The waiting room had steel benches, and a solenoid lock clicked to admit me into the nurses' station. File cabinets, phones ringing, people walking purposefully. This was more like it.

A slight man with close-cropped hair popped out of an exam room and pumped my hand. "Adam McIntyre," he announced. "You've got to be Dr. Wright."

"Got to be," I agreed.

Adam was an eight-year CDOC veteran after giving up a hectic private practice.

"It was eating me alive," he said. "I had more and more administration and less and less time to actually see patients. The last round of payment cuts did me in.

"This way I don't have to pay for an office or hire staff, somebody else gets the administrative headaches, and I don't have hospital politics to deal with. I don't get to call the shots like I used to, but when I clock out, I leave it all at the office."

Adam gave me the tour of the Fremont clinic. Several of the room layouts were weird compared to a normal office. The physician's desk blocked the examination table and his chair faced into the room from the side of the desk nearest the door. "Never let an offender get between you and the door," Adam said. "Always keep the door open and the way out clear."

"You mean..."

"Sometimes they're having a bad day. Best not to become part of it."

He sat me down at his desk and demonstrated the CDOC computer system. Electronic medical records were all the rage. After seeing the responsiveness of the system, rage might have been an apt description.

"Has it locked up?" I said.

"No. This part always runs a little slowly. It depends on the time of day." I stared at the stationary cursor. We could have gone out for coffee before the next screen appeared.

"It's a pig," I said.

"Oink," he nodded. "It's just been upgraded. Now it runs slower than before, but at least it crashes more often."

"More often? That's a feature?"

"Every time it crashes you have to reboot. The computer guys say it helps clean out the system.

"That's the first phone number you'll learn. Just dial HELP. We wanted the extension to be SHIT, but administration already had that one."

Fremont clinic was a lot more freeform than CSP. No handcuffs. No escorts. Offenders walked in and out of the waiting area but were still called back individually through a locked gate to the nursing area. From there they went to the doctor's office.

Adam went to the nursing station to get his next patient. I thought that was a nice personal touch and complimented him.

"I come to get them so I can walk behind them on the way to the office," Adam said. "Never turn your back." So much for civility.

He did a few patient examinations and data entries to show me how it worked. "I'm very problem-focused here. One complaint per visit. Otherwise they'll keep after you with problem after problem. They get charged a co-pay for every appointment and they want to cram in everything they can think of."

"What's the co-pay?"

"Three bucks."

"Wow. I can see how they would want to stretch it out. Three whole dollars for a doctor's appointment."

"And free drugs and follow-up appointments."

"Sounds like a medical program that could only be conceived in Congress."

"Better plan than we've got," he said. "Then there's chronic care."

"Which is?"

"For chronic diseases like high blood pressure or diabetes, its three bucks for as many appointments as you need for a whole year."

"And drugs?"

"Free"

"Surgery?"

"Free. Free room and board too."

"Any chance I can sign up for this plan?"

"Sure. Just kill somebody and turn yourself in. Of course, there's always the chance you'll be rooming with Bubba."

"I knew there'd be a down side."

FOUR

ON MY OWN

E very fledgling gets kicked out of the nest eventually. My training and orientation complete, my first day as an unescorted, unchaperoned, untested CDOC physician arrived.

I turned at the correct spot on US 50 this time and pulled up to the East Cañon Complex guardhouse. The CO waved me through with only a perfunctory glance at my ID. I was all set to get frisked, but I could have just held up my library card.

The hulking brown mass of CSP crouched on the right. I announced myself to the squawk box, ran the gauntlet of catcalls from the day hall windows and pushed into the front lobby.

I collected my tote bag from front desk security and strode into the main sally port like I knew what I was doing. As the door clanked shut behind me, I had just enough presence of mind to sign in and exchange my monogrammed metal chit for a set of restricted keys. Seven keys on a sealed cable ring. What were all these for?

The inner door of the sally port opened and I entered the labyrinthine main hallway. No signs anywhere. Left? Right? I think we went right on my orientation with Sabrina. Pretty sure we went right. Probably the only thing worse than being in a supermax prison is being lost in a supermax prison.

A blue uniform appeared. "You lost, Doc?"

"Well, yes, a little. Which stairway to get to medical?"

He pointed down the empty hallway. "Down there to the right. Keypad's by the door."

After fumbling my key card to open the stairwell door, I descended the two flights to the basement. Locked door. There's a button. Push? Don't push? I waited, but the door stayed impassively closed. What was it Sabrina said? Stairwells were OK to push—or was that the sally ports?

What the hell. I pushed the button and heard the solenoid buzz, releasing the lock. Guessed right for once.

Past the lower control station to the medical clinic door. Wait. Don't push the button. Door finally opened. Two right guesses in a row. Into medical, turned right down the hall to the door marked *Physician*. Which of the seven keys opened this? The last one.

My office was a comedown from the cushy days in private practice. A twelve-by-twelve concrete block room featured a wired safety glass window with a view of the concrete block hallway. Florescent fixture. Wall clock with dangling electrical plug. An L-shaped desk half-filled with an antique computer and printer. Linoleum floor. A cheap secretary desk chair. Wall cabinets containing obsolete manuals, forms, and handouts. A cork board filled with extension numbers of departed employees. A bookcase with thick binders of Clinical Standards and Procedures. A steel sink with an automatic shutoff faucet like you find in gas stations.

I sat down in the midst of my new domain. I couldn't get my legs under the low desk. The chair didn't adjust. A layer of dust coated the shelves. In a fit of domesticity I grabbed a paper towel and punched the faucet. A spray of water erupted. I wet the towel and went to work on the top layer of grime covering the desk and shelves. The water kept running. And running.

I banged the faucet, hoping to shake the recalcitrant valve loose. No go. I now had a water feature. I found that the faucet would shut off after about five minutes of water gushing into the thin steel sink.

I gave the maintenance guys a call. When they ambled by, I showed them the sticking faucet. "Yep. Some of 'em do that," they agreed. "Can't fix it without tearing the whole thing out." That wasn't going to happen.

Since the chair was immutable as well, I asked them to cut a couple of two-by-fours to fit under my desk and jack it up enough for me to sit down. Now there was a project they could handle! Quicker than you can say "Union Labor" the desk rose four inches and I could breathe.

With the water off, the place was filled with the hush of desperate stone. Only the persistent hiss of the overhead ventilation made any impression on the silence.

I had wrangled permission to bring in a CD player and a stack of disks. No iPods allowed. No internet music. That was probably just as well. If I tried to stream music over this network, it would be playing one...note...at...a...time. But the CDs were enough to keep me from going bonkers.

I didn't have a window to the outside, so I put up the largest calendar I could find featuring outdoor scenes. I brought in some of my art and slapped it on the concrete walls with Velcro dots. I was home.

A nurse popped in. "Clinic starts in twenty minutes, Dr. Wright."

<hr>

He'd killed five people in cold blood. Three men and two women gunned down with a cheap .38-caliber handgun in a suburban fast-food restaurant. A wiry black man, really almost a boy, slouched on the gurney with studied indifference as I took his blood pressure: 110/65 with a pulse of 60, the same numbers a person might register if he was asleep. My numbers were considerably higher.

"Whatchu want with me?" he sneered. "I ain't put in no kite to see you. I ain't payin' for this."

The shackles on his legs rattled as he shrugged to adjust the handcuffs linked to the chain padlocked around his waist. The two guards inched forward, alert for sudden violence.

"Just a routine check," I muttered. I felt as if touching my stethoscope to his chest might be like lighting a dynamite fuse.

He cocked his head, a sly grin spreading his thin lips. "You scared, ain't you doc? You should be. I be the baddest man you ever see."

I didn't answer. *What the hell was I doing here?*

FIVE

EXPLORING

My first clinic session completed, I ventured out to get acquainted with the facility. Approaching the door to the staircase I had descended earlier, I found no wall speaker and no button. There was a plastic panel sticking out, however. "Hello?" I said tentatively. I heard a knocking behind me and turned to see an officer in the glass-enclosed control area pumping her ID card up and down and pointing at the wall beside me.

Ah! I pulled out my card and held it next to the panel. The solenoid holding the door buzzed open. Cool.

I climbed four flights of stairs to the main level. With only a little hesitation I pushed a button on the landing and the door popped. Wow! I was getting the hang of this.

After negotiating four more flights of stairs and the sally port into the B-Pod wing, I checked out the medical room set in the corridor wall. Instead of a keypad, it had a regular doorknob. Locked.

I pulled out my gaggle of keys but none came close to fitting the large keyhole. I glanced down the corridor to the central hub. I could see officers circulating in the control area above the office. One paused and looked down at me. He waved and the exam room door buzzed open. So that's how it's done! I waved back and entered my dominion.

The medical exam room in B-Pod was stripped to essentials. The cinderblock walls were painted a pastel pink while large glass windows faced the control center and the hall. The color scheme might have been psychologically soothing according to some guideline, but still came across as something from a Pepto-Bismol commercial. An air vent conducted the cadence of an offender counting off calisthenics to his neighbors. Posters with information on hepatitis C in Spanish and English were the only décor.

A stainless steel column combining a toilet, sink, and drinking fountain huddled in a corner behind a half-height cinderblock wall. A sign over the fixture declared, "This is not a toilet." Maybe it was like the call buttons that weren't used to call anyone.

A sheet of roll paper hung disconsolately over the end of a standard examination table. An otoscope and ophthalmoscope hung on the wall next to a blood pressure cuff and scale. Not exactly high-tech, but at least the basics were covered.

Except supplies. Where were the supplies? Tongue depressors, alcohol swabs? Ah, must be in the locked wall cabinets. I fished out my ring of restricted keys. Here's one that looks like it might fit. Nope. Another. And another.

As it turned out, some keys fit none of the locks, some keys fit locks in exam rooms on other pods but not this one. Some keys opened one cabinet but not the one next to it. Several locked cabinets were empty. Some cabinets couldn't be opened at all. You could spend all day just trying to find a cotton ball. I decided to bring my own stuff from the main clinic in the basement.

I turned to go. The door was locked again. I peered through the window facing the control center but couldn't see anybody looking my way. I waved. I waited. Surely they'd be watching for me. Surely...

Five minutes passed and not a friendly face appeared. Finally a CO came out of the sally port and walked by the exam room. I knocked on the glass. He smiled and pulled out his more impressive ring of keys, quickly opening the door. "We always use a doorstop," he said. "Easy to get locked in." No shit.

C SP has a PA system. Maybe it's because of my aging ears, but the announcements sound like pronouncements of an asthmatic duck. At first I assumed that an urgent announcement in a prison might be something you'd want to pay attention to. It turns out that the more urgent the announcement, the less important it is.

The speaker blared, "ASURJO:KLPFSDRE!!!" I went around the corner to the nursing station. "What was that on the PA?"

"It's either a total structural collapse of A-Pod or it's count time." She looked at the clock. "It's count time."

The same goes for alarms. Again, I thought, alarms in a prison are to be heeded. Well...

The CSP safety officer is a man who loves his job. His job is to set off fire alarms. All of them. Constantly. If there was ever a real fire, someone would have to go door-to-door and inform staff that *this* time they needed to get the hell out.

His job also includes maintaining MSD sheets. These are Material Safety Description sheets that put forth in agonizing detail the chemical composition and potential lethality of everything liquid, solid, or gaseous that passes through the door. Everything. I can see it for dangerous chemicals, but a jug of diet Arizona green tea? What are the chances?

A Rs or administrative regulations make up the bible of the prison. These are the rules that cover every conceivable occurrence within the confines of the prison grounds. There are lots of 'em. You want Budget Preparation Procedures? Right there in AR 100-02. How about Parole Violation Process? AR 250-41 has it covered. Want to know how somebody gets out of the slammer? AR 550-11 tells you all about Offender Release.

They go on endlessly (to 1600-03 as of today). And, of course, I'm supposed to be familiar with all of them. The inmates certainly are.

The can quote them word-for-word, editing and twisting the content to fit their particular agenda.

Because of being surrounded by AR scholars who have nothing better to do than look for loopholes in the rules, I frequently spend my chart review time looking up the specific AR that covers the issue in question.

Fortunately for me, medically related ARs always start with 700. If an inmate rants that I've violated AR 450-02, which covers "Payment Procedures for CDOC Goods and Services", I immediately know he's just upset that he got charged for a medical appointment and can blow it off. If he picked an AR like 700-12, I'd have to actually go look it up. 700-12 covers "Birth Control, Pregnancy, Child Placement and Abortion," so I don't have to read beyond the title to know he's got the wrong one.

Every month emails arrive from administration inviting me to read proposed ARs and comment on them. Needless to say I don't open these for fear a twenty-page markup document will clog my printer. Still, somebody has to do it. Just not me. I suppose this is how democracies fall to ruin.

C DOC is enthusiastic about email. Especially after a weekend, I can count on a whole page full of items of urgent importance. When I first came on board CDOC I read everything, thinking that if someone in the prison sent email to me, it must have some relevance to me or my job.

"URGENT!!" says the title, so I pop it open. "Sonya Eggers will be out of the facility until tomorrow," says the message. Who the hell is Sonya Eggers, and why should I care where she is? Why is Sonya concerned that I be able to locate her? Is this some sort of enticement that maybe I should look her up tomorrow when she returns? Sadly, the message leaves these questions open.

I get emails about Chris going on vacation, Marla thanking all her friends for the flowers, results of monthly fire inspections and rescheduling of escape team meetings. All of these would be more fascinating if I knew any of these people or if I was involved in any of the fire inspection or escape teams.

You want to know if inmate Smith is up for a parole hearing? I got an email on that. Interested in whether a case manager is being reassigned? I'm informed.

Of course, to keep junk out of my mailbox, CDOC has a dandy spam filter that deletes all the medical newsletters and professional communications I've indicated I really want to get. It even has a feature that asks if I want to receive the item it has marked as spam next time it's sent. I do. It deletes it anyway. Keeps the mailbox clear for notification of Betsy's anniversary.

A special kind of email sneaks in occasionally. It's "Secure Email." I think it comes from a facility in Denver. I'm not sure because it's so secure that I can't open it. You need a password to get a password. Not worth it. I figure they'll call if it's something important.

SIX

SAY AAH

I figured that my background as a surgical specialist would come in handy with prison medicine. I'd seen the shows. Knifings. Shootings. Beatings on every hand. A wonderland for a trauma surgeon.

What I found was a kind of third-world general practice. High cholesterol. Stomach aches. Back pain. Asthma. High blood pressure. It hadn't occurred to me that these tough, battle-hardened criminals might also have regular human diseases.

I got to sew up an occasional cut, usually self-inflicted, but for the most part I cared for the same kind of diseases any general practitioner might see, using the same intellectual tools physicians have used since the first witch doctor shook a rattle. With one important exception: history.

The most important tool a doctor has in his diagnostic arsenal is the patient's history. One of the first axioms drilled into a new doctor is, "Listen to your patient, he is telling you the diagnosis."

It's true. In the world of private medicine I could learn more by just shutting up and listening to my patient than I could from a raft of MRIs, CT scans, and multi-gallon blood workups. But not anymore.

Now patients who lied about anything and everything surrounded me. I quickly found that I couldn't depend on a single thing they told me.

A common tool in assessing pain is the one-to-ten scale. It helps quite a bit to know if abdominal pain is a two or an eight. At CSP all pain is at least a ten. And then the pain gets worse. Hard to make much out of that.

Another medical truism covers this situation: "It is much more important to know what sort of patient has a disease than what sort of disease a patient has."

What the inmates lacked in imagination, they made up for with suggestibility. I learned to stick to the subject at hand and not ask about general health issues. If I mentioned it, the inmates had it.

- Chest pain? Oh, man. All the time, Doc. I need some Motrin or something.
- Short of breath? Terrible, man. I'm gasping just getting out of bed. It's the altitude. Can I get a lower bunk?
- Stomach upset? With the food here, I puke my guts out. I need some of that Prilosec stuff like you gave Jones.
- Hangnail? Pure torture, Doc. Got 'em on my toes too. It's these boots. I need special shoes.

I wondered about these street-tough gang lords who staggered into the clinic whining about their chronic low back pain and heartburn. If they were this incapacitated while sitting around doing nothing, how did they ever pull together enough strength to commit a felony?

So instead of knife wounds I saw much less exotic emergencies. For example, if there's one thing that's endemic at the supermax, it's constipation. Bobby White, a rapist from Grand Junction, visited me a while back.

"Jesus, Doc, I ain't shit in two weeks. Ya gotta do somethin'."

"So how much water are you drinking, Mr. White?"

"I'm drinkin' all the time. Day and night. Gallons!! I'm pissin' every ten minutes."

A quick check of the urine shows it's so concentrated, it looks like Tang. He probably hasn't peed since Christmas.

"Water, Mr. White. You're constipated because you aren't drinking enough water."

"No way, Doc, I need—"

I interrupt, holding up a finger. "Water is the magic word, Mr. White. You're not drinking enough to keep a gnat from being constipated."

"You think?" he says, amazed at my clinical acumen.

I nod sagely. Another life saved.

I like to start off a new inmate exam with an open-ended question that lets him tell me what the most pressing problem is. Usually I'll ask "What's going on?" or "What's up?" Most people would take that as a cue to tell me why they're visiting me today. Most people.

It's amazing how many inmates can't remember why they're seeing me. These are the same people who had previously sent kites with "EXCRUCIATING PAIN!!!, THINK I'M DIING!!!, "NEED AMEDIAT HELP!!!"

Xavier Melon, a sometime gang enforcer from Denver, sent me such a kite.

"So Mr. Melon, what's up?"

"Uh, is this about the acne?"

"No, it's about the excruciating pain, going to die."

"Oh, yeah."

"So...?"

"Can I get something for my bowels? I ain't shit in a week."

"What about the excruciating pain?"

"Yeah. I need some stuff for that too."

When I saw Richard Gillis, a murderer of three business associates, I had to convince him that he was sick.

"Mr. Gillis, what's happening?"

"Beats me."

"So, what are we getting together for today?"

"I dunno. You called me down."

"You sent me a kite."

"I did?"

I waved the kite. "Yep."

"Lemme see it."

"Here you go. Ring any bells?"

Gillis handed the kite back. "I didn't send that."

"Hmm. It's your name, your CDOC number, your pod address, and your signature. Your secretary screw up?"

"Oh, yeah, I remember now. It's all gone."

"All gone?"

"Yeah. Can I get something for my bowels? I ain't shit in a week. I ain't gonna get charged for this am I?"

Adrian Boyce, a general bad-ass on loan from Arizona, was so used to keeping information close to the vest that I never did find out what his problem was.

"Mr. Boyce, so what's going on?"

"My kidneys."

"Your kidneys."

"Yeah."

"Could you expand on that a little bit? What about your kidneys?"

"You know. It's my kidneys."

"So your kidneys are causing you some kind of problem?"

"Yeah."

"And that problem would be...?"

"You know. Kidney problems."

"Problem kidneys, eh? Maybe if I slap them around a little bit, you think they'd shape up?"

"I dunno. You're the doctor. Can I get something for my bowels?"

———

The medical staff at CDOC was often the first health care professionals the inmates had ever seen. It's understandable. Most of our guests were more likely to get shot than die of high cholesterol. In any case, the gangs didn't have great health insurance.

Often this meant I had a lot of educating to do. That was okay with me. I'm a frustrated professor, and I tend to give my patients more information than they want or need. The problem is that inmates are better at talking than listening.

I saw Elvis Vialpando, a wife-beater and newly diagnosed diabetic. I spent ten or fifteen minutes explaining to him what diabetes is and how we could manage it.

"So does this make sense to you?"

"Sure."

"Any questions I can answer for you?"

"Can I get something for my bowels?"

It seemed to me that Vialpando had missed a key point—that he had diabetes and it could cripple or kill him. I backed up and gave him the executive summary on diabetes for another two minutes. I sat back, pleased with my cogent, illuminating presentation.

"So they'll start testing your blood sugars tomorrow."

"What for?"

"To see if we've got you on the right dose of medication."

"You gonna start me on medicines?"

"Yes. It will start to bring your blood sugar down."

"I got sugar in my blood?"

At this point it's clear I was wading in the shallow end of the gene pool. My emphasis shifted from education to administration. I leaned closer to Vialpando's placid face.

"Tomorrow the nurses will bring you a pill. You will take it. They will prick your finger before breakfast and take a drop of blood. Don't worry about it. I'll see you next week."

"OK."

I really should give up the education bit, but it's something ingrained in me. In private practice, when things didn't work out as predicted it was often because the patient didn't understand the nature of his disease and why we were doing what we were doing to control it. At CSP, it seemed like shoveling smoke. I'm afraid my best intentions to educate ended up like the adult voices in a Charlie Brown special—*wa-wa-wa-wa*.

In most cases I don't think it's because the inmate was stupid. He just had a different agenda. He was coming to see me not because he wanted to control his diabetes or high blood pressure, he wanted some pain medication. Or something for constipation. Or a thicker mattress. Or special shoes.

So he tuned out everything that didn't lead him to getting the things he really wanted. He'd listen politely, his mind somewhere over Omaha, until he heard a key word that he could seize on to further his real desire. Here's a non-sequitur from a recent visit with Richard Keller, a chronic alcoholic and purveyor of stolen property.

"When you're on this medication, Mr. Keller, you can't just stop it all at once."

Keller, who had been lapsing into a stupor, suddenly brightened. "That's what I mean, Doc. I'm all stopped up. You got to get me somethin' for my bowels."

"What's this medicine got to do with your bowels?"

"You just said it, Doc. Stoppin' is bad. You gotta help me."

Inattention sometimes reaches gargantuan proportions. I was seeing Keith Pollock, a drug trafficker, about his prostate problems.

"Mr. Pollock, has anyone done a rectal exam in the last year or so?"

Pollock looked as if I'd just asked him to explain the Electoral College.

I forged ahead. "You know. The doctor puts on a glove, lubes it up and sticks his finger up your butt to feel how big the prostate is."

Despite a look of intense concentration, Pollock comes up blank. "I don't remember."

"You don't remember if somebody stuck his finger up your ass?"

Pollock shrugged.

E xamining patients was a little different in prison than it was in private practice. There were some obvious differences like not having to validate a parking ticket, but there were others as well.

Communication with my private practice patients was usually straightforward. I'd shake hands and introduce myself. They would tell me reasonably clear medical complaints like, "I can't hear very well anymore" or "I've been dizzy for a week."

The most important part of a medical encounter in private practice was taking a history. People who are paying good money to sit in your exam chair usually have a fair idea of why they're there. Prison was different.

From the outset, I couldn't shake hands with someone handcuffed behind his back. I had to make do with "I'm Dr. Wright" and let it go at that.

The reason they appeared in my examination room was often unclear. I might get a kite that simply says "Sick" or "Want to see a doctor, not that other bitch." Inmates often had trouble elaborating beyond that. Marvin Hamilton, an ex-boxer and thief from Pueblo, was a case in point.

I sat on my exam stool looking at a kite that says "Sick." I did my standard opening gambit: "So, Mr. Hamilton, what are we getting together for today?"

"I dunno. You called me down."

I held up the kite. "Sick?"

"Oh. Yeah."

"What kind of sick?"

Hamilton looked mildly annoyed at my lack of comprehension. "You know. Sick."

"I don't have a checkbox on my form for 'Sick.' Could you be a little more specific?"

Hamilton was obviously getting pissed at this boob of a doctor that couldn't grasp the obvious. "Sick, man. You know."

And so it goes. If I was really curious or had time on my hands, I might have expended the effort to drag out his actual complaint. I pretty much knew at this point, however, that there was nothing wrong with Hamilton, and he'd forgotten why he put in the kite.

"You ain't gonna charge me for this?"

"You bet. Three bucks and worth every penny."

"Shit."

That pretty well sums up the encounter. Of course, rarely, there actually is something wrong with Hamilton or his cohorts. Then I could swing right over to the physical exam, which presented its own set of challenges.

Unless I happened to see a Goth, most of my private patients weren't in chains. It's tough to take a blood pressure when the patient's hands were cuffed behind his back. For the same reason, I couldn't examine the abdomen when the patient can't lie down. How do you evaluate a painful shoulder when I can't move the joint? It was hard to hear heart sounds when the CO's radio blared at my shoulder.

There were tricks to get around some of these limitations. I could have the COs switch the behind-the-back cuff restraints to what is called a "strip out" configuration where the handcuffs are attached to the belly chain by a separate short length of chain on either side of the body. This allows more freedom of motion and access to arms for blood pressures and shoulder joints for evaluation. Also, they can lie down on the exam table if there is something of interest in the abdomen to check out. Likewise, I could have the COs remove the foot shackles to check the legs independently.

The drawback of these kinds of maneuvers was they took time to do and undo and they put everyone, including me, in more danger of a sudden attack both during the switching of restraints and while the inmate was more mobile.

In spite of these restraint variations I still had to go on instinct and experience. History was usually poor because the inmates frequently lied, had limited descriptive ability, and very little intuition about health in general. One of the most frequent comments I got when an inmate didn't like the treatment I prescribed is "I know my own body," but they seldom did. What that meant to them was "I can beat you up" or "I can bench press 400 pounds."

Most inmates got used to being constantly on display, but privacy was an issue for some of my charges. There were always at least two COs in the room with us and they might be of either sex. This could generate some awkward moments. Ralph Noble, a rapist, was unaccountably shy in the presence of female COs.

"I got a... you know," Ralph mumbled.

"Not really."

"You know. A rash or something."

"Where?"

"You know."

Now I did know. What happened next depended on whether Ralph had irritated me enough in the past to let him off the hook with the two female COs hovering next to the exam table.

If I felt charitable, I'd just say, "Let's have a look." If Ralph had been misbehaving, I'd come back with, "What? You got a rash on your penis?"

In either event, the next step was to drop Ralph's drawers and check it out. This was even more fun for him if a rectal exam was involved. Hands cuffed behind his back, butt hanging out and me sticking a finger into his nether regions while the COs tried to look impassive. You had to have a little sympathy even for the jerks.

After the physical exam was done, we came to the explanation of what's going on. It gave the expression "dumb it down" a whole new meaning. We're not talking about explaining the effects of diabetes on the kidney. Ralph doesn't even know he's *got* a kidney.

On the other hand, some inmates are really into their diseases. These are the ones I spent the most time with undoing the misinformation they've accumulated from television commercials, their relatives, or their outdated copy of *The Home Health Guide*.

The law of inverse results came into play. The more information presented, the lower the understanding on the receiving end. It was much more effective to cut to the chase and say "You've got diabetes. Take this."

Then comes the denouement. I've done a great job of diagnosing the disorder, prescribing the treatment, and educating the patient. My work here is done. Not. Here's recent exchange with Tommy Grimes, a breaking-and-entering specialist from Colorado Springs.

"So I'll see you back in a couple of weeks to see how the program is working."

"What about my back pain?"

WILLIAM WRIGHT, M.D.

"Back pain? I've just spent twenty minutes teaching you how to manage your blood sugar."

Grimes shrugs painfully. "My back's killing me. Can I get a thicker mattress? And I need something stronger for the pain."

"What about your diabetes?"

"I got diabetes?"

Ah, well...

SEVEN

I Need That Green Pill

Inmates have an inborn talent for denial and doggedness in pursuit of their goals. I saw Cecil Schroeder, a chop shop entrepreneur from Fort Collins, seeking pain medicine.

"My foot hurts."

"You had a fracture of your heel ten years ago. You've got more screws than Home Depot. It would be a second-order miracle if your foot didn't hurt."

"Yeah, but it hurts."

"You need a new foot. We're out of stock. What is it you want?"

"My knee and back hurt too."

"The way you walk puts strain on your knees and back. You need to use the heel pad and quit limping around. At CSP you only need to walk from your bunk to the cell door. What, eight feet tops? You could fall down and still make it."

"Yeah, but they gave me some stuff at Limon that helped a lot."

"I'll bet they did. You're at CSP now. You can get pain medicine from the canteen if you want it."

"Don't do no good."

"So you want me to give you more of what don't do no good?"

"I need some of that..." (thinking hard) "What was it??" (This is a huge red flag. Whenever an inmate is trying to think, it means he's lying.)

Schroeder's face contorts with concentration. "P... something. Per... Per..."

I couldn't stand the suspense. "Percocet?"

Schroeder brightened. "Percocet! That's it. It really helped a lot. Can you get me some of that? Just for a while. Just for a few months."

"No. Use the heel pad. Have a nice day."

"But you—"

"Elsewhere."

Another distinction from private practice is the variety of complaints. One curve ball I received was from an inmate who sent a kite saying "my beed implants have slipped." I couldn't wait to see this.

It turns out that he'd had four glass beads implanted under the skin of his penis "for the enjoyment of my companion." One had migrated out of line because of some scar tissue and he was concerned about it.

I'll admit that as a Midwestern farm boy I'd never seen anything quite like it. I guess I need to get out more. From a medical standpoint there was nothing to do except reposition the errant bead when he got out of jail if he wanted it to line up properly.

Other kites are just as intriguing. One winner said, "Please check my oil level in my body. I put oil in my Body Lawfully Christianily, The Church."

This promised to be something novel, but it turned out that he just had dry skin. So I told him his oil level was indeed low, and he needed to add some via a skin lotion he could get at the canteen. I didn't ask how the church figured into this.

Examinations are times for non-sequiturs. Wanting to get the most bang for their three-buck visit, inmates usually jump from one symptom to another like nymphomaniacs at a Viagra convention. Tanner Evans, a carjacker with asthma, sat in my clinic.

I placed my stethoscope on his back. "Take a big breath through your mouth."

"I got warts on my dick."

"Congratulations. Just take a deep breath."

"My sister says I could have high cholesterol. My father had high cholesterol I think. Can you check me?"

"Just a deep breath. Don't talk."

"Sorry." (millisecond pause) "This rash..."

I held a finger in front of his face. "No talk. Just breathe."

"Okay." (starts humming the theme to *Star Wars*)

Another characteristic of examinations was the infallibility of friends, relatives, and television. I got a lesson on this from Roy Wilkins, an arsonist from Walsenburg.

"Joanie says I need treated for diabetes."

"And Joanie is...?"

"My sister. She's got a friend with diabetes and says I need treated for that."

"You don't have diabetes."

"She says I do. She read up on it."

"I did too. You don't have it."

"How do you know?"

I pointed to the chart. "Because your blood sugar is normal, your kidney function is normal, your eyesight is normal, and your physical exam is normal."

"You guys are all the same."

I've found that an outside authority helps a lot to bring about consensus during exams. One of the best is Google. It saved me recently with Sean Ruddell, a hypochondriac thief from New Mexico.

"I know it's cancer. You're lying to me. You don't know shit."

"Actually, I'm very familiar with shit. What you've got isn't cancer. It's just a benign cyst. Benign means not cancer."

"You just don't want to fix it."

"You're right about that. It doesn't need fixing. It's a benign cyst."

"Like you know."

I brought up Google Images on my computer and tapped a few keys. "Here's a picture of what you've got. See the bump there. It's a benign cyst. Says so right there."

Ruddell studied the screen with ferocious intensity. "That's it?"

"That's it."

"Okay."

I could have shown Ruddell a picture of damn near anything because he's conditioned to believe anything he sees on a screen. Now he thinks I'm brilliant. Thanks, Google.

At CSP the inmates have lots of free time to watch television. Like medical students coming down with every disease they study, inmates come down with every disease they see on the tube. Harvey Downing, a murderer and sometime preacher of the gospel, sent me a kite with the single word, "Pill."

"I need that green pill."

"Could you be a little more specific?"

"That green pill they got on TV."

"Oh, *that* green pill. And we would be taking it because...?"

"You know."

"I must have missed that episode. What's the problem that the green pill is supposed to fix?"

"You know. I can't pee."

"Ah. So when's the last time you peed?"

"About a half hour ago."

"Fixed! You can pee."

"No, I mean I can't pee sometimes. Like on TV. Like those old guys."

"You're twenty-two."

"Right."

"So when can't you pee?"

"You know. Like when I work out and I forget to drink water."

"In the medical profession, we call that normal."

"But that green pill. I know it'd help a lot."

"Next."

Another characteristic of CSP inmates who have sent a kite and spent their three bucks is they not only want the perceived problem fixed, they want it fixed NOW!! Typically the problem is minor and has been present for years. Darryl Foster, a petty thief who graduated to grand larceny, sent me an urgent kite: "Cancer!! Urgent!!" I could hardly wait.

"I got this growth on my arm. It's cancer. You gotta get me to a hospital and get it cut off now."

"How long has it been there?"

"Since I was in Territorial." Inmate time is frequently measured by dates of incarceration and different prisons they attended.

"I haven't been following your career. That would have been about...?"

Now Foster is under the gun to come up with an actual date. He shrugged. "I guess maybe '94 or '5."

"And this has suddenly exploded?"

"Well, yeah. It's gotten a lot bigger. And it hurts. Excruciating."

I flipped through the chart. "Here's a note from ten years ago. Same thing. Same location. Same size."

"Well, it's gotten a lot bigger. I need it off now."

"Not to mention the pain."

"Yeah. The pain. Constant. Excruciating."

"It's a lipoma. A lump of fat under the skin. It's been there forever. It's not getting bigger. It's not cancer. It doesn't hurt. It doesn't need to come off now or ever."

Foster became indignant. "What the hell do you know? I want to see a real doctor."

"No problem. Read AR 700-21 (I have it memorized). It tells you how to see an outside doctor. Of course, you'll have to pay for it."

"I'm filing a grievance!"

"Everybody does. Have a nice day."

Another variation on the "I want it fixed now" are the guys who start on a medication that takes a month to kick in. No matter how much conversation we have about what to expect from the medicine, it's inevitable that the next day I'll get a kite complaining, "This stuff is shit. It don't work at all. I need that stuff I told you about on TV."

Of course the stuff on TV takes a month to kick in too, but that's in the fine print.

The inmate concept of a medical emergency is a little fuzzy. You and I think of an emergency as something that comes up suddenly and requires immediate attention—like a heart attack or a severed artery.

Not so in prison. A medical emergency means they've got nothing better to do that day. Ozzie Winslow, a maker of keys to other people's safes, sent me an emergency kite saying, "Need to be seen today!!"

"So Mr. Winslow, what's the emergency?"

"Pain. I got pain, Doc."

"Any particular spot?"

"All over. It's terrible. Excruciating."

"Wow. I'll have to say you look remarkably composed for a guy in excruciating pain. How long have you had it?"

"About three years."

"No kidding. It's a wonder you've made it this long."

"You said that right, Doc."

"So what's changed?"

"It don't change. It's there all the time."

"I mean what makes it an emergency today?"

"Well, you brought Jones over. I figured you ought to check me out too."

"What's Jones got to do with it?"

"We work out together. He's in court today. He can't work out with me. So here I am."

"You're working out with Jones?"

"Yeah. We're having a contest. See who can do five hundred push-ups fastest."

"In excruciating pain."

"Right."

Another characteristic of the emergency visit is an increased level of impatience for results. Conrad Tobias carried it to an extreme.

A CO poked his head into my office. "Dr. Wright, Mr. Tobias is declaring a medical emergency."

"It's okay. I just saw him fifteen minutes ago. All squared away."

"No, he's declaring *another* medical emergency."

"About what?"

"He says he still has the pain."

"He hasn't even had time to get the medication yet. It won't be in until this afternoon."

"He wants to be seen again."

"It's good to have goals. Next."

EIGHT

KITES

O ffenders make their medical needs known by sending a note to medical with their complaint. These notes, called kites, contain space for two lines to outline what the problem might be. Something like, "Stomach pain" or "Woke up dead."

It seems the offenders take it as a challenge to their compositional skills to cram a complete medical history on the two lines. The theory is that sheer volume makes up for any lack of sense. Keeping in mind that we had few college professors incarcerated at CSP, the literary skills of the majority were limited. Spelling was optional.

"IgotaHUGEbumporsomethingonmyleganditsgotalotbiggerthis morninganditreallyhurtsBADandIgotagetseenRIGHTNOW!!! Thank you"

Almost universally the intensity of the demand for immediate treatment is tempered by a humble "Thank you" at the end. And I'm sure it's meant sincerely, that is, until I say no to whatever remedy they had in mind.

The form for the kite had a line for "Work Assignment." This was meant for the general population prisons where the inmates actually had assigned jobs. Nevertheless, the CSP residents got into the spirit of the thing. Some examples of their "Work Assignment" entries:

- Prison Skills
- Unemployed Outlaw
- Retired Burglar
- Working on Six Pack
- Student
- Life of Leisure
- Body Builder
- Anger Management
- Vacation

The Hispanic inmate kites were more challenging. Not only were they not in English, often they weren't in Spanish either. A typical kite might read "Mi angustia se deriva de mi loro." Translated literally this comes out as, "My anguish flows from my parrot."

I speak Spanish, but many of the Hispanic kites are head-scratchers. Spanish is a phonetic language, but these guys mumble when they spell. Most of the time I just assumed they wanted an appointment and sorted it out later.

Usually the small things got the most attention. I didn't get many kites requesting adjustment in cardiac arrhythmia therapy. Constipation, acne, stuffy noses, dry skin, or the multitudes of back, neck, shoulder, knee, and foot pain are what drew the crowds.

The inmates had a constant preoccupation with their testicles and bowels. It seemed everyone spent most of their day on the can ruminating about how slow their intestines were moving. Presumably while they're sitting there on the can they noticed this lump on their testicles and panic set in. Fortunately they're in the best location possible to receive this sort of bad news. The bowel problem frequently resolved at the same instant.

Raphael Dominguez was a guest at CSP due to a carjacking gone wrong. I received his kite filled with exclamation marks about the cancer he'd discovered in his testicles.

"So, Mr. Dominguez, what's up today?"

It's tough to shuffle your feet when shackled, but Raphael managed it. He glanced furtively at the two COs, one a female, who accompanied him to the exam room. "I got a lump," he mumbled.

"No kidding? Where might this lump be?"

Squirming in his belly chain, he gave a little head toss. "You know."

"Ah, you mean your testicles?"

"Yeah, you know."

Slipping on a pair of exam gloves, I rolled my stool over to him. "Let's take a look."

His eyes swiveled toward the COs again. "Right here?"

"Spa's closed today. Drop 'em."

A quick exam revealed a benign cyst rather than the cancer he was sure he had.

"It's good. Just a cyst. A little collection of fluid. No problem."

His fear morphed suddenly to suspicion. "Not cancer? How you know it's not cancer? I think it's cancer. You just don't want to pay to fix it."

"You're half right. I don't want to pay to fix it. The good news is that it doesn't need to get fixed. I know it's not cancer because I've seen a boatload of 'em. Not cancer. Good to go."

"Not cancer?"

"Nope. Sorry."

"I can still, you know..."

"Father scads more children? Unfortunately, yes."

"While I'm here, can I get something for my bowels?"

No matter how small the complaint, inmates want the million-dollar workup. I got a kite from Ed Rhoden, a counterfeiter, reading: "complete physical, HIV, hepatitis and all other blood tests and total body MRI scan and so on." His problem? He didn't have one, but was "just checking."

Kites often are just fishing expeditions. Franz Epstein sent: "I have AIDS and I need some kind of pain medication." Of course, Ed didn't have AIDS and had no condition requiring even an aspirin. Apparently he didn't think I was sitting there with his medical records in front of me. "You have AIDS? My God, get this man some oxycontin right away!!"

One fishing expedition kite from Jonas Stamper, a serial rapist, read: "A Doctor. I still have an aching, undiagnosed shoulder, kidney? or liver? Or bladder: or spleen? Seriously, I need an MRI, something is wrong, somewhere and it won't 'Go Away.'"

This would have been funnier if it hadn't been Jonas's third kite about the same thing. I gave up explaining why he didn't have any of these problems and just wrote "Issue already addressed" on the kite and sent it back. It's a contest of sorts. If my reply was shorter than the complaint, most eventually gave up.

Don Morales, a whiney little whippet incarcerated for child moles-tation, was notorious for the third kite trick. I answered kites in order of submission unless there was some catastrophe that needed tend-ing. Morales sent in most of his kites with the bold heading "THIRD KITE!!" before proceeding to the demand de jour. His intent was to make me feel guilty about missing his previous requests for help, mak-ing it more likely that (1) he would be bumped up to the front of the line and (2) I'd compensate for our neglect by giving him whatever he wanted. He never seemed to realize that I had records of all the kites coming through and knew this was his first on this particular subject. It usually got him bumped to the bottom of the stack.

Some of the kites were destined to be counterproductive. Here's a classic: "Who do I kite to see somebody who knows what the hell they're doing? Not that bitch nurse or that dummy asshole doctor!" Gee, not even a "thank you" at the end. Still, kites like this were so outrageous that they're funny and kind of lightened the day. A little.

Inmates used kites to try to "split" prison staff, to turn one mem-ber of the staff against another. They've been told "no" by one person, so they ask the same question to somebody else, hoping for a different answer. Then it's "But, Dad, Mom said I could do it!" If the ploy works, they've got the staff disagreeing with each other with an increased chance that the inmate will get what he wants. Double-cuffing was a frequent splitting issue.

Double-cuffing meant using two linked pairs of handcuffs to cuff an inmate instead of the usual single pair. Since inmates were almost always cuffed behind their backs, double-cuffing was more comfortable, but also more dangerous for the COs and anyone else in the vicinity.

Some inmates were so large that the COs routinely used double-cuffing because they physically can't get their arms close enough behind them to use one pair. That's fine and that's the CO's choice.

The red flag went up when I got a kite from inmate Masters complaining he had excruciating shoulder pain and wanted me to tell the COs to use double-cuffing on him. He wanted to split us, me against the COs, but I called him down to the exam room to check it out.

"So I see here that you're in excruciating pain. Tell me about it."

Masters was momentarily at a loss, trying to remember what his kite was about. He recovered by grimacing and limping to the exam table. "Oh, yeah, Doc. My knee's killing me. Horrible. I need something strong for it."

"Oops," I said.

"Oops?"

I held up his kite so he could read it. "Oh, yeah, the shoulder too. It's worse than the knee. I need those double cuffs."

I did an examination of the distressed shoulder and knee. Masters was obviously into bodybuilding. I made some notes on my clipboard and casually asked, "So what kind of exercise you doing now?"

Inmates have a point of pride about their exercise capacity. Masters, forgetting himself again, brightened. "Pushups, dips, burpees, some chins in the dayhall."

I put on my best buddy face. "How many can you do?"

Warming to the subject: "Usually about 700 pushups, but I'll get to 900 sometimes."

"No kidding. What about the burpees." Burpees are a combination of pushups and squat thrusts.

"A few," he said modestly. "Maybe 200 or so."

"Can you guess why your shoulder and knee might hurt?"

"I dunno. You're the doctor."

"I'll give you a hint. If I did over a hundred pushups, my arm would fall off."

"Well, maybe so, but I been doing this a long time. I know my body."

"Say hello to your shoulder and knee. No double cuffs. Back off the exercise."

No split. The COs and I stayed on the same page. Unless there was a good medical reason for it, and that almost never occurred, I never overruled the COs' call on security issues. The COs were the people who had to take the risks attendant to handling these guys and were in the best position to make the calls on safety.

Splitting attempts often occurred with medications. My first patient of the day, Raphael Gonzales, wanted pain medicine for his aching back.

"You gotta get me something for this back. It's killing me."

"Devoutly to be wished," I muttered.

"Tichner said he'd get me some T3, but he never put it in. That Motrin doesn't do shit. Can you just put the T3 in for a few weeks?"

T3, Tylenol with codeine, is almost never used at CSP. I checked back to the note from Tichner, the PA, and found to no surprise that he recommended a course of physical therapy instead.

"It looks like Tichner wanted you to get started on some physical therapy."

"Yeah, well that and the T3."

"He seems to have left that part out of his note."

"He was in a hurry. Probably just forgot."

"No T3."

"No T3? But he said—"

"I'm thinking not. Maybe you heard him wrong."

"What about the Motrin at least?"

"I thought you just said it didn't work at all."

"Maybe just a dose increase."

"So you want more of what's not working?"

"Well, yeah. I mean it was working a little bit."

"Do the PT exercises like Tichner told you. You can get the Motrin off the canteen."

"But I got no money for canteen. I'm insurgent."

"Close. Maybe you're indigent," I said, pulling up the computer screen again. "Wow. Looks here like you've got $158.43 in your account. You should be taking me out to lunch."

"No way. I got nothing in the account."

I tapped the screen and turned it for him to see.

"No shit. Somebody must have just put that in there."

"Fairy godmothers in the supermax. It's a miracle."

Inmates also tried to split the CSP medical staff using outside consultants. One kite was from an inmate who had been out for a routine colonoscopy: "Don't need to be seen! Do Not Charge! The Gastroaligest in Pueblo told me to tell you's if I need'ed another Bental in the mourning to help with my guts & stomach! So it will be two a day - Please order one more for the Mourning - a Bentel. Thank you."

The gastroenterologist, of course, said nothing of the kind. This guy was just fishing for some additional pills to sell or snort. Bentyl was a perennial favorite for this, although I've yet to see the reason for the attraction. Snorting Bentyl should be about like snorting chalk, but I guess I shouldn't knock it if I haven't tried it. It's just part of the prison drug mythos.

It seems cliché that hardened criminals go to prison and "get religion." I've found an inverse relationship between religious conversion and trustworthiness. Not that any of these guys are trustworthy, but it just seems that the more they thump the Bible (or Torah or Qur'an), the more I have to watch my back.

If you take the time to look up their offenses, this is a group with more than its share of child molesters and axe murderers. "Comin' to Jesus" or the equivalent doesn't seem to arise from any sense of remorse for past deeds. It's more a justification for acts—present, past, and future. "God commanded me to (fill in the blank)." It's also a power trip since now they're "enlightened" and everyone else is a deluded moron. With divine justice on their side, they're free to lie, cheat, steal, and beat the living crap out of anyone who gets in their way. And they do.

It's especially true for the new converts. When I get a kite that says, "Have a Blessed Day!!" I know there's trouble coming. It's a lot like "Thank you" at the end of a rant, except the implication is that the writer is not really asking for himself, he's merely communicating God's wishes. And woe be unto him who does not honor God's commandments. Most of the time that would be me. Alan Yellowstone, a guy in CSP for accidentally murdering three people who owed him money, visited my clinic two weeks ago.

"Mr. Yellowstone, I notice you've been refusing your blood pressure medicine."

"Yep. Don't need that shit anymore."

"And that's because...?"

"Found Jesus, Doc."

"And Jesus is going to fix your blood pressure now?"

"I'm healed, Doc. Washed in the blood of the lamb."

"Today the lamb's blood pressure is 160/110. That's stroke territory. You want to rethink this?"

"Numbers don't mean nothin'. I'm pure. I'm healed. I can feel the spirit movin' within me."

"That would probably be the aneurism pulsating in your head."

"Glory to God!"

"Hallelujah."

When an apostle gets wound up in the clinic, feverish with the spirit upon him, I have an almost irresistible urge to smack him on the forehead and cry "Heal!" I'm not sure the COs would catch him as he fell backward though.

As it is, I'm often the bearer of bad karma. Where most of the time I get anger and attitude, with the Religious Right I get moral outrage. As chief philistine I'm forcefully reminded of my spiritual bankruptcy and threatened with divine retribution. Here's an exchange with Steve Cedrick, a collector for one of the Denver gangs and recently the recipient of a mail order divinity degree.

"What's up today, Mr. Cedrick?"

"That's Reverend Cedrick."

"My mistake. I didn't recognize you without the robes. So what are we getting together for today?"

"I need a new mattress. I bet you wouldn't give Jesus a mattress like I got."

"If Jesus was doing twenty-five for aggravated assault, I sure would."

Cedrick tried to make the sign of the cross, but was brought up short by the belly chain. "Blasphemy," he intoned. "I pray for your soul."

"Thanks. I can use all the help I can get."

Fortunately Cañon City has few lions prowling about to pounce on non-believers, but I keep looking for frogs and locusts in my car at the end of the day.

NINE

THREE BUCKS

Inmates are only allowed one complaint per kite and therefore one issue per medical appointment. Since an appointment cost three bucks, the inmates wanted to squeeze the maximum out of the visit.

Donny Mosciano, a car thief from Alabama, knew how to work the system. His last kite said, "I tore up my knee and it hurts BAD. Thank you." Sounds pretty straightforward.

When I saw Donny in the clinic, he limped up to the exam table, grimacing and nearly in tears from the horrible pain. I would have been more impressed if I hadn't seen him practically skipping in his shackles on his way down the hall.

Tapping the knee, I looked into Donny's moist eyes. "Does it hurt in here, Mr. Mosciano?"

"Ow! Jesus, Doc. That hurts like a son-of-a-bitch! And I got these warts or something on my arm. Whadda you think? And I been havin' this trouble peeing. Up all night."

"One catastrophe at a time, Mr. Mosciano. What about your knee?"

He looks as if he didn't quite understand the question, then suddenly remembers why he came in the first place.

"Yeah, man. Hurts like a mother right there (wherever I happen to have my hand at the moment). You gotta fix it. I need something right now. I had this at Fremont. They gave me something, fixed it right up. I forget the name. P-something. Par. Per. Percocet. Yeah, that's it. Percocet's what they gave me." He put on his best just-helping-you-out-Doc face.

"Not happening."

"But they—"

"No, they didn't."

"What about peeing all night?"

"Send me a kite. We'll look into it."

"But I'm here right now. You could check it out."

"I could check out my stock portfolio too, but right now I'm concentrating on your knee."

I finished up with the knee exam and explained the disorder and the treatment. Donny wasn't giving up.

"This rash is driving me crazy."

"Sounds like a mental health issue. If it's bothering you, just send me a kite."

"But—"

I nodded to the officers. They escorted Donny from the medical suite along with his knee, rash, nocturnal peeing, chronic pain, and fifty other complaints that he didn't get to voice.

Now this sounds like a stupid system at first blush. Why not take care of all the problems at once and be done with it? I tried that for a week or two when I was first on the job.

One problem is that having nothing to do 24/7, the offenders are acutely focused on every burp, bump, and itch their bodies produce. Many obsess about ailments and abnormalities so minor as to defy detection. The demand for medical services is huge just from the standpoint of something to break the monotony. Enter co-pays.

When medical services for inmates were entirely free for the asking, they asked. A lot. CDOC then instituted a co-pay, mostly as a triage mechanism. If you thought the fight over a trillion-dollar health care package in Congress was fierce, you should experience the daily moaning and bitching about the cost of prison medical care. It's a rare appointment that doesn't include the plea "You ain't gonna charge me for this are you?"

The three-buck cover charge does indeed discourage some of the frivolous complaints from reaching me. But these are crafty guys. The major ploy to avoid paying for the visit is "The Follow-up."

When I need to see someone back for another visit, I'll schedule a follow-up appointment for him. He doesn't get charged for this visit because I'm the one who wanted to see him again. If he wants to see me, that's an appointment and he gets charged.

Nosirrah Reynolds was a heavily built redneck in CSP for aggravated assault on a street cop he thought was seeing his sister. Scrawled on the front of the chart in bold letters was, "Call him Rocky." He limped into the exam room and struggled to the table. I couldn't help myself.

"Nosirrah. I don't ever think I've seen that one. Middle Eastern?"

"Kentucky," he growled. "It's Harrison spelled backwards. My folks were big fans of the Indiana Jones movies. It's a crock of shit."

"Ah. Well, Rocky, what's up today?"

"My back. Can't sleep. I need another mattress." He locked eyes with me. "I ain't gonna get charged for this."

"Actually you're already charged. It's an appointment."

"They seen me for this at Territorial. It's in the chart. Same thing. It's a follow-up."

"This isn't Territorial. I haven't seen you before. You asked to come. Three bucks."

"I've had this for years. It's chronic care. A follow-up."

"Nope. Appointment."

"Fuck it. I ain't gonna pay."

"Already done. You're here. It's an appointment. So tell me about the back."

Forgetting his excruciating pain, Rocky sprang off the table to get in my face. "I ain't gonna pay for this. This is bullshit! This is a fuckin' follow-up!"

"It's not. You've already been charged the co-pay. Do you want—"

Rocky launched his considerable bulk at me as best he could with the cuffs, belly chain and leg shackles. I caught him by the shirt as we fell backwards into a counter. The COs had Rocky on the floor before he could bite me.

He spit on my shoe. "Shit! Fucker! All you fuckers are the same!"

"His back seems better," I said to the COs. "Appointment's over."

Another follow-up ploy was the revisit of a previous outcome the inmate didn't like. Albert Simmons, a forger from Cincinnati, was perennial at this.

"So what's the problem today, Mr. Simmons?"

"My knee. I can't walk on it."

"Instant cure. You just walked in."

"I mean hardly."

I shuffled through the chart. "Ah. You saw the PA for this last week."

"Yeah, I need a follow-up on that."

"He didn't call you back. How do you get follow-up out of that?"

"My father had a bad knee. Runs in the family. This should be free, chronic care."

"Did your dad sprain his knee jumping from a second-story window too?"

"I just want my Motrin. The PA forgot to put it in."

"Not according to the note. He discontinued it because of your ulcer."

He gave me a stare of cement-like incomprehension, turning quickly to anger. "I need that Motrin, not that crap Tylenol that don't do nothin'."

"Motrin is not on the menu today. You got the Tylenol. If it's not helping, I can take you off of it."

"You ain't gonna charge me for this. I didn't get nothin'."

"But it was a nice try."

"You fuckers are all the same, bleeding us dry."

"It's a grand medical tradition. Leeches and all."

"Shit."

In their defense, I have to remember that many only get "state pay." This means they get a base pay of twenty-three cents a day from the State of Colorado up to a maximum of $5.29 a month. This is compensation for committing a major felony and sitting in a cell all day. On balance, it doesn't leave a lot of discretionary income.

Still, when I check their canteen purchases, it's amazing how many seem to find cash for beef sticks or jalapeno squeeze cheese, but can't afford an aspirin for their excruciating pain. A matter of priorities.

———————

I t's amazing what magnificent physical specimens emerge from the inmate population. With no exercise gadgetry at all they can turn out bodies the envy of anyone at Gold's Gym. Who needs equipment? They've got time.

All these guys come from populations where it pays to be fit. You might even say it's critical. Like ex-marines who carry the fitness ethic all their lives, the inmates of CSP raise fitness to the level of religion.

They do endless calisthenics. Not dozens of pushups and pull-ups. Hundreds. A burpee, a combination of a squat thrust and pushup, is a favorite. Crunches? Thousands. Usually they work out about five days a week, some for an hour, many for two to four. Some never quit.

They make weights by rolling up their mattresses or lifting books or legal boxes filled with papers. When somebody orders *War and Peace* from the library, you can bet it's for the extra weight. They have regular exercise times with leaders calling out the cadence for pod members.

There's always a price to pay. Many of the chronic pain problems, especially backs and joints, are due to overuse and stress injuries. It's an odd position for a physician to tell a patient to cut back on his exercise, but I do it all the time.

Adrian Lenox, an Aryan supremacist, is a calisthenics leader on A-Pod. Every afternoon at two o'clock on the dot, he drops to the floor of his cell and starts calling out a cadence for pushups. He keeps this up for an hour before graduating to crunches and other calisthenics.

"You gotta give me a shot for this shoulder pain, Doc."

I examine Lenox's arms, each the size of my thigh. "Looks like you work out, Mr. Lenox. About how many pushups do you do?"

Lenox puffs up. "About eight or nine."

"Really. I would have thought more."

"Jeez, Doc, nine hundred pushups at a set is pretty good. I do a couple sets a day."

"Ah. Nine hundred. That sounds more like it."

"Damn straight."

"Time to cut those back a bit."

"Cut back? I been doing this for years."

"That's why your shoulder's giving out. Tendonitis from overstress. Give it a rest."

"Maybe cut it in half for a couple days?"

"How about cutting it out for a couple of weeks. Then we'll shoot for a number that's humanly possible."

I had an inmate complaining he'd had chronic fatigue for ten years. He worked out two hours every day. Cardio. Weights. The whole bit. He was in great shape but was as dehydrated as someone crossing the Sahara. Often people forget that Cañon City is in the "banana belt" of Colorado. Higher than Denver at over 5300 feet, sunny and arid. Just hanging around doing nothing requires a lot more water intake than most areas of the U.S. When you're doing two-hour workouts, the fluid requirement skyrockets.

When an inmate comes in complaining of fatigue and multiple joint pains, my first question is not, "Have you visited sub-Saharan Africa recently?" More likely I'll ask "How many pushups are you doing?" If the answer is in four digits, I've got the diagnosis.

———

S itting around all day can get you focusing on your body. Tiny things that wouldn't even reach consciousness in the real world become horrendous issues in the prison population.

Pain? Don't get me started. In the real world a pain scale is a valuable tool in diagnosing and treating illness. How bad is the pain on a 1-10 scale? One is barely noticeable. Ten is blindingly agonizing, wanna-die pain. If a woman with kidney stones breaks both legs falling down the stairs while delivering a baby, that's a ten. So what are we talking about here?

At CSP the pain scale starts at ten and goes up from there. A splinter is a ten. A stubbed toe is eleven. It's amazing how an illiterate population can come up with words like "excruciating," "torturous," or "agonizing." And, of course, "You gotta give me something for this. Right now. Thank you."

It seems the last prison they attended treated these complaints perfectly. "I don't know, Doc. They were giving me those blue pills. Fixed it right up. I forget the name. It was something like "oxygen" or "oxy-something." Furrows of deep concentration line his forehead. He squints, trying to remember the name of the mysterious drug. Light dawns. "Oxycodone. That's it. Oxycodone. It worked real good."

First of all, the guy never got oxycodone at the last facility. He hasn't seen oxycodone since he partied with it on the street. He's probably got a crate of it in his garage.

Second, it's a dead giveaway when an inmate comes in asking for a specific drug. It almost always means he's abusing it in some fashion. Most of these guys can't remember the name of the disease they have, let alone the medications used to treat it.

So here's Lionel Riddle, a drug dealer with an abrasion on his hand. He got it by punching the concrete wall in his cell. Ten times. I couldn't resist.

"Mr. Riddle, why did you punch the wall?"

"I was pissed, Doc."

"At the wall?"

"I do that sometimes."

"Who sold you on that strategy?"

"Nobody sold me nothin'. I just need somethin' for the pain."

I resist the temptation to ask how bad the pain is. It's hard to listen to them try to pronounce "excruciating."

"I'll get you some Motrin for a few days until you can get some from the canteen."

"I need something stronger than that. How come I can't get some Percocet?"

"You're in prison."

This seems to stymie him for a moment, but he quickly recovers.

"But I got Percocet at Limon."

"In your dreams. Motrin or nothing."

"Okay. I'll take it."

"You know, in the future you might avoid this by not punching the wall."

This provokes an indignant glare.

"Not my fault."

"Hard to see how it could be, but the next time the wall attacks you, just call a CO for help instead of trying to fight it out all by yourself."

He considers this, rubbing his hand. Finally nods.

"Might."

———

The tremendous advantage of experience in any field is that you know what's normal. The bullshit meter is much more finely calibrated.

How do inmates counter this bulwark of science? *The Home Health Guide.* Prisoners have copies of this or similar books and can glean the symptoms of whatever disease they might like to have at the moment. Howie Karlgren, a freelance bad-ass from downstate in Walsenburg rocked back and forth on the gurney, grimacing and holding his belly.

"I got this pain right here, Doc," indicating his right upper abdomen. "It's been a lot worse when I eat fried stuff. And you know my shit? It's like this clay-color. I think I need an MRI. And something for this pain."

By now the meter is pegged. Inmates make the mistake of being too classic. Too pat. It never happens like that in the real world. There's always a layer of ambiguity on top of the solution to the problem.

"So, Mr. Karlgren, this only happens when you eat fried food?" You can see the sweat percolating, wishing he'd read his Cliff Notes a little more carefully. *Whatthefuck man! This wasn't in the book!*

"No. It happens other times too."

In a perverse way, I'm beginning to enjoy this. "Like when? How about when you lie down?" The noose tightens.

"Yeah. Sometimes." The wheels are coming off the wagon.

"And it kind of burns when you pee?"

"Yeah. Kinda."

"Notice a sort of red rash that comes up on your feet at night? Itches?" Now he's beginning to wonder if he's *really* got something bad.

"Not sure about that. I mean, I'm kind of a heavy sleeper."

"Some headaches in the morning right about here?" putting my finger to his temple.

"Oh, yeah, man. That's part of that pain I'm talkin' about."

"That's good news."

"What's good news?" He's cautious again.

"Well, for a minute I thought you might have a problem, but with what you've told me it looks like you'll be fine."

"Fine. I ain't fine, man. I'm sick. I got this gallbladder thing and you gotta fix it. I need something for this pain." He thinks about going for excruciating but decides he can't pull it off.

Detective Colombo strikes. "Gallbladder thing? What page is that on?"

He's blown. He looks over at the escorting officers and back at me. He lets go of his belly.

"Shit. You ain't gonna give me nothin'."

"Right. See you later."

This does not mean that I don't get suckered on occasion. I had an inmate declare a medical emergency. When he came to the clinic he seemed extremely agitated but in no real medical distress. The emergency problem? He was allergic to wool.

It seems that the cotton blankets, which had been in the housing units, were being replaced with wool ones. It's January in Colorado after all.

This inmate spun a great story about a lifelong allergy to wool, complete with the mere mention of the fabric bringing on anaphylactic shock. There was no mention of this malady in his prior medical record. Okay. In a moment of weakness I said he could have his cotton blankets back until we figured out the wool allergy angle.

By the clock, within five minutes of his return to the housing unit there were six additional medical emergencies being declared for wool allergies. Oh, fudge. If my old HSA was still around she would have grinned and reminded me that no good deed goes unpunished.

CSP inmates have absolutely no sense of humor. In any other working environment I've experienced, patients were able to lighten the load with some kind of humor. Not here. At CSP it's just grim.

That's been a real adjustment for me. In my private practice, humor was a valuable part of the communication process with my patients. If I acted like a problem wasn't necessarily the end of the world, my patients could step back and get a little perspective on it too. At CSP I quickly learned that the inmates take everything I say very literally. Jerry Lather, a grand larceny convict from Denver, was one of my early mistakes.

I looked over Lather's sheet of vital signs. "Wow! If your blood pressure was really this high, we'd be taking you to the ER."

"I ain't goin' to no ER."

"No. That's not what I meant. See this number? The nurse wrote it in the wrong place. It showed your blood pressure was over 300. Just a mistake. I'll fix it."

"So I gotta get my blood pressure fixed? Is 300 too high? I ain't goin' to no ER."

"No. That's not your blood pressure. It doesn't need to get fixed."

"It's my blood pressure. The nurse just took it."

"She wrote it down wrong. Your blood pressure is okay."

"Nurse always had it in for me. Tryin' to kill me."

This is why stand-up comics don't play Cañon City.

A unique feature of prison medicine is that failure is not an option. The concept that a pill might not relieve every physical ailment is as foreign as feathers on a walleyed pike.

Larry Sago, a murderer from Limon in eastern Colorado, apparently threw his back out while disposing of a body. One of the risks of the trade.

I'm seeing Sago for his chronic low back pain for the fourth time. I've been through all the exercise routines and medications we can use. It's crunch time.

"Doc, you gotta fix this!!"

"Mr. Sago, there *is* no fix for this. The best thing is for you to drop a hundred pounds and start doing the back strengthening exercises."

"You don't understand, Doc. This hurts BAD! You gotta fix it."

"Actually, I don't gotta fix it."

Sago was incredulous. "I'm a ward of the state. You gotta fix it."

"No. All I really have to do is keep you alive. I'm not in the comfort business. Take some responsibility. Lose the weight. Do the exercises."

"It's not my fault. You gotta fix it."

"It's not your fault? Somebody snuck up and stuffed a hundred pounds of lard in your mouth while you were asleep? Get real."

"You ain't gonna give me nothin'?"

"I've got nothing to give you for this. The magic truck missed its delivery this week."

"You ain't gonna charge me for this, are you?"

"Special tax for dumb. Three bucks." I don't really say this, but ohh-hh do I want to.

When inmates disagree with the way they've been treated, they can file a grievance. In a grievance, an inmate has most of a whole page of paper to set out the injustice he's suffered along with his requested remedy. It's a legal process, not a medical one.

I like grievances. If a kite is a derringer of annoyance, a grievance is a howitzer of outrage. You get a sense of the full scope of their thinking and, for the most part, it's pretty bizarre.

The inmates have learned certain buzzwords to drop into grievances. "Deliberate indifference" is a favorite because it's an issue that can legally get providers into trouble. We don't have to be right all the time, but we can't be deliberately indifferent to the poor inmate's plight.

Many grievances are laced with references to legal cases or administrative regulations, AR's, which purportedly prove their assertions of injustice and neglect. I got one from Bob Hickman, an unemployed welder and car thief from Denver, who accused me of violating "The Fairness in Medicine Act which guarantees my in-Alienable right to negotiate this co-pay." Of course there is no Fairness in Medicine Act. If there was, I'd be sipping margaritas on my yacht surrounded by nubile supermodels. That's what I call fair.

I can't speak to the legal references —"Rack v Slub, 1983, Colorado Court of Appeals"—which are usually misquoted and have nothing to do with the inmate's complaint, but the references to ARs are usually the kiss of death for the grievance.

ARs are the rules of the prison. They spell out in agonizing detail exactly what everyone can and can't do. It's quick work to look up the pertinent AR and see which part is being misquoted, distorted, or just fabricated.

Some grievances are just howls of outrage because the inmate didn't get what he wanted. Here's one from Ashanti Lincoln, an extortionist who used to do hits for hire: "I got this excruciating pain in my shoulder that keeps me awake day and night for the last 500 days. I need a complete blood workup, x-rays, and MRI and other scans and an orthopedic surgeon instead of these quacks you got here. I been sending kites twice a week and nobody answers them and medical is being deliberately indifferent to my needs. And I want $200 a day for the pain and suffering until I get the proper care and get this fixed."

As you might guess, Ashanti has been seen umpteen times for his excruciating shoulder pain. He neglects to mention that he's been told to back off his eight hundred daily pull-ups and is pissed because he can't get more pain pills for recreational use and barter.

But I still think it's fun to read these diatribes because of the red-hot emotion that singes the edges of every page. These guys will go to the mat trying to get their three-dollar appointment fees refunded or to complain about a nurse who called their petulant bluffs during medline. They rant and scream about their rights and how the courts have mandated that they receive extra food, a thicker mattress, or some type of elective surgery.

Like most lies, grievances contain a grain of truth, but the grain is usually buried beneath a truckload of distortion and hyperbole. Here's an excerpt from an inmate who didn't like fish and wanted to have a special fish-free diet. The spelling and punctuation is above average for what I usually get:

"I got document's that states clearly that food tests (known as RaST test) is not recommended for Food cytotoxic testing, Because it is NOT proven to Be accurate or safe, and that was proven by the Fedral Register on June 13th of 1985."

The grain of truth is that a RAST test is not 100% accurate for food allergies. Everything else in the statement is bullshit.

Here's part of another:

"I'm filing this grievance as an 'emergency grievance'; because there is an indication of potential/substantial risk to my health and/or to my life!"

Wow! Sounds serious, eh? His request was to be taken to the hospital by ambulance so someone could check his hemorrhoids.

It's common for inmates to act like everyone is out to get them. True as this may be for some of our guests, we of the CSP staff try to behave ourselves. Nevertheless, this issue sometimes shows up in grievances:

"Torture. CSP staff still continue to Torture me by spraying poisonous chemicals into my only air supply. The only purpose of This sadistic and malicious Act is Plainly clear. That purpose is to cause me Death and/or serious Harm."

Spraying chemicals through the ventilation system is a popular fantasy. I've got a handful of inmates who are absolutely convinced the

CSP staff is putting mind control or toxic fumes into their vents. If only we could...

"It the better part of a year that CSP medical clinicians have denied my serious medical need. The medical team at CSP knows of these toxic assaults and when I've gotten solid proof of them thru the clinic – medical staff has done everything in their power to conceal the truth by denying and changing past toxicology tests."

I had to ask this guy why, if he'd been inhaling poison gas for a year, wasn't he dead or even sick? Were we that incompetent? I never should have opened that can of worms. "So you admit it!!"

As a rule of thumb, if you don't get sued at CDOC at least a few times a year, you're probably not doing a very good job. The longer you're there, the more likely you'll be the target. It's mostly because you get better at saying "No." I usually counted on about one suit a month. I was on a first-name basis with Robbie, the process server. He knew my schedule so he'd come in the evening, and we'd have him in for coffee.

One month I was sued twice in the same week. Since the inmates usually can't find an attorney willing to file on the kind of issues they want litigated, they file their own suits. After all, they have nothing but time.

The first suit that month was about getting the wrong size shoes. It's often hard to tell exactly what the suit is about, since the unlimited length of the complaint format allows them to vent ad nauseum. It's like a grievance with infinite paper.

The second suit was about an inmate not getting a walker. This particular guy ended up at CSP because he *did* have a walker at another prison and used it to assault a CO.

He was contending that, for no particular reason, he couldn't walk and needed a wheelchair. I remember seeing him in the clinic and not finding any reason why he needed anything at all. He got mad, got up, and stomped out of the exam room, dragging the COs along in his wake. Despite his miraculous recovery, apparently he held a grudge.

As stupid as these lawsuits sound, it's a little unnerving to see your name on the Defendant line of the summons. The awards requested always start at a million bucks and go up from there. I don't give them much thought once the initial shock subsides. But then again, this is America, and you can get rich spilling coffee in your own lap.

TEN

AN EAR DOCTOR FROM INDIANA

How in the hell did I end up as a prison doctor? When I drag home after a day of hostility, tension, and insults, I've asked myself the same question.

I have a medical heritage. My great-grandfather made horse-and-buggy rounds to his Indiana patients. My grandfather and father specialized in ear, nose, and throat. The writing was on the wall for me, but I wanted to be an engineer.

I was always a geek. Math, science, I loved them. I built my own parabolic mirror for a science project. I thought logarithms were neat. I was even in the high school slide rule club. You just can't get geekier than that.

When I looked at medicine, it represented dealing with the imprecise problems of people rather than the elegance of equations. No contest. When relatives asked what I wanted to do when I grew up, there was no doubt it would be something in the applied sciences. Then came German.

In my high schools days of the early '60s, a great deal of the engineering technical material was only available in German. I'd have to learn the language if I wanted to be a player, but I could barely squeak by in elementary Spanish. No way was I going to learn German. I took another look at medicine, where I could at least use a language I knew.

Much to my parents' dismay, I gave up a full-boat scholarship to the engineering program at Rice University to enter the out-of-state-tuition world of a pre-med program at the University of Michigan.

I roomed in an apartment with three engineering students. The biology courses started off innocently enough, but soon I was dissecting fetal pigs and dogfish sharks on our Formica dining room table. Cat skulls were in short supply for a comparative anatomy class, so I procured a corpse from an experimental lab and left the skull on the roof of the apartment building for a few weeks.

It's every bit as gross as it sounds, but the maggots did a great job of cleaning the skull for me. My roommates finally fled when I evicted the larvae with boiling water in the bathtub.

My older cousin, Don, pestered me through high school to come to a little dirt-strip airport with him to learn to fly. Finally giving in on a warm Indiana afternoon, we each took an introductory ride in a Piper J-3 tail dragger. I was hooked. Don lost his lunch and never flew again.

Throughout my undergraduate years at Michigan whenever I could scrape enough money together for a lesson, I'd hitchhike to the Ann Arbor airport for a spin in a Cessna 172. I ran out of money and time before I soloed, but I put getting my license on the bucket list.

Michigan had an early admissions program that allowed entry into the medical school after three undergraduate years instead of four. I knew my grades were OK, but the competition for U of M medical school was fierce. Since they gave preference to Michigan residents, I didn't think I had much of a chance since my home was in Indianapolis.

I scheduled an interview with Dr. Whitehead, one of the medical school admissions physicians. He asked all sorts of questions about what books I liked to read, what extra-curricular activities I participated in, and so forth. Since I'd spent most of my time studying to get enough credits for the three-year program, I could tell that my sparse resume did not impress him. There was a great deal of pencil tapping and half-frowns until he asked if I played any musical instruments.

I'd played the sousaphone, the huge horn that wraps around your body, in my high school band. Dr. Whitehead perked up. Inexplicably, he loved the sousaphone. He went on about how John Philip Sousa developed it for use in his marching bands in the 1890s. He was an encyclopedia on Sousa and his music.

The upshot was an acceptance letter in my box a few weeks later. I was going to be a doctor because I played the tuba. Only in America.

Medical school was the prototypical marathon of long hours and no money. I married my high school sweetheart and moved in with other medical couples down the hill from the hospital in what was prophetically dubbed Fertile Valley. My first daughter, Jane, came along a couple of years later.

Aside from bridge and beer parties on weekends, social life in medical school was almost non-existent. Pestered by the wives to get us out of the house, a group of Fertile Valley med students joined the glee club. I can't sing now, and I'm pretty sure that I couldn't then either, but if enough voices belt out a tune it sounds impressive if not exactly musical. It must not have been too bad, as we sang at the med school graduation.

In the first two years of medical school at the University of Michigan I got lots of theory but very little opportunity for application. As a third-year student I was allowed to touch a patient only if medical school staff personally supervised me. In retrospect, this was a wise policy, yet I was feverish to put my new knowledge to the test. But where? In the pristine halls of Ann Arbor's hospitals? Not likely. Detroit wasn't so picky.

The Saturday Night Knife and Gun Club met in the Motor City every weekend. Our little clan of medical students was hot to participate. Primed with hours of practicing surgical knots to practical use, a group of us took the hubcaps off our cars and headed to Detroit Receiving Hospital in the inner city. This was my introduction to patients being chained to gurneys. At CDOC I found I'd come full circle.

Detroit Receiving felt a lot like CSP does now. Surrounded by cops, we'd sew up the various lacerations that rolled through the door. Urgency was in the air. Our patients wanted us to patch them up fast so they could go wreak the same havoc upon whoever put them there. Slow learners, just like the CSP crowd. Maybe some of them are my patients now.

On my first trip I was paired with an intern. We were present-ed with an inebriated woman who had lost a knife fight. The intern grabbed two suture kits and handed one to me. He went south to the cuts on her stomach and indicated I should start on the facial wounds.

I popped open my kit, struggled into the surgical gloves, and fum-bled a sterile barrier over my assigned area. I found the needle holder and tore open the pack of suture.

I realized that although I knew how to tie a square knot, I'd never actually put a needle through skin and gotten a suture in position to tie it. It looked so simple in the book.

Although it doesn't look that way on M*A*S*H reruns, suture nee-dles are delicate little devils. I maneuvered my needle holder over the curve of the suture needle and deftly bent it into an unrecognizable pret-zel. Nervous and semi-humiliated, I opened the holder and watched the needle and attached suture slide off my carefully prepared sterile drape onto the floor. The intern looked up quizzically. I shrugged. "Slippery."

His eyes narrowed. "Done much suturing?"

"Not too much."

"Any?"

"Well, actually, no. This is my first."

He nodded and elbowed past me. "You do the belly. I'll do the face," he said.

———

As a newly-minted MD fresh from medical school, I knew a lit-tle bit about a lot of things. A year of internship taught me that the world of real people with real problems was a lot messier than the neat diagrams in medical books. This was old school medicine, work-ing 16-hour shifts, with many occasions of working 24 hours and then another 16 on top of that. It was the most exhausting, scary, and ex-hilarating time of my life. I had people look at me and ask, "What do you think, doctor?" *Doctor.* They were talking about *me.* I actually used my knowledge to make a difference in other people's lives. Very heady stuff.

As a bonus, I was getting paid instead of shelling out tuition. Five thousand dollars a year plus a ham at Christmas. In addition, I got a tiny apartment next to the loading dock of the hospital, so I was instantly available if needed. I'd never felt so needed in my entire life.

In later life I saw television specials about the training for SEAL teams. Weeks of no sleep with superiors constantly yelling conflicting instructions and demanding peak performance at all times. Bunch of pussies.

After my year of internship I was a real doctor in the eyes of the law. I was legal to hang up my shingle and be a soldier in the war against the dark forces of death and disease. Specializing sounded attractive, so I began looking for something I thought I might be good at.

In my case I knew I wasn't any good at dermatology. Skin diseases all looked like red blotches to me. I couldn't diagnose measles. Too much screaming in obstetrics. Pediatrics was okay, but not quite where I wanted to spend my career. Internal medicine was a possibility, but it seemed that the diseases never really went away. High blood pressure. Cholesterol. You could patch things up for a while, but then the dike would start leaking and you'd have to plug the same holes all over again.

That pretty much left surgery. It appealed to my sense of "fix it and be done." I thought a long time about emergency medicine for the same reasons, but ultimately the lure of the knife drew me in.

So I was off to a year of residency training in general surgery. At first I assisted senior surgeons doing appendices, gallbladders, and hernias. I learned how to cut and stitch on minor cases.

Like so many things in life, surgery looks pretty easy when someone accomplished is doing the work. I'd held retractors and closed skin incisions for the senior surgeons while they did the more intricate procedures. I'd seen so many appendectomies I was sure I could do them in my sleep. Until...

Marshall Smith was a general surgeon of the old school. Meticulous. Correct. Kindly. A true Marcus Welby clone with a soft southern accent. The kind of surgeon you want when it's your life on the line.

I'd done several procedures with Marshall where I was doing my year of general surgery residency at Tampa General Hospital. As we came in from the scrub sink and donned our gowns for the third surgery of the day, Marshall said, "Why don't you do this one?"

In later years I would have the same feeling when my flight instructor got out of the Cessna 172 we shared and said, "You take it up."

For those of you not familiar with this feeling, it's called panalysis, a combination of panic and paralysis. But then I thought, *How hard can it be? I've watched and assisted with dozens of these cases. I can do this.*

There's nothing quite like the feeling when, as an apprentice surgeon, you have a real live patient in front of you and your mentor hands you the scalpel. I looked at the virgin abdomen, orange from the Betadine scrub, concealing the traitorous appendix. Suddenly I realized I had no idea where to make the incision. I'd seen it in books. I'd watched other surgeons do it almost casually. Where was the dotted line?

I looked up helplessly at Marshall. His eyes crinkled behind his mask. Without a word he drew a linear smudge in the Betadine with his gloved finger and looked away. It was my case.

My scalpel tentatively traced Marshall's mark. A miniscule red line of blood followed my path. I cut again, thinking of all the vital organs lying just beneath my blade. The streak of blood was incrementally larger, more like a scratch than an incision.

Marshall blotted the tiny line of blood. "We're going to be here a long time if you're going to scrape through the skin one cell at a time," he commented dryly. I flushed furiously, took a deep breath and finally made the incision.

We sat in the surgeon's lounge after the case, my scrubs still dark with sweat. Marshall sipped a cup of his favorite herbal tea as he dictated the operative report in his soft southern drawl. I was still too much into my adrenaline high to take anything but a shaky drink of water from the wall fountain.

Marshall contemplated the mid-distance for a time and finally smiled. "Don't worry, Bill, you did fine." He put a veined hand on my shoulder. "Welcome to the club." I was a surgeon.

Not all physicians were the caliber of Marshall. As I walked down the main corridor of Tampa General, an ear, nose and throat surgeon,

Doctor X, stopped me and asked, "Do you want to assist me with a surgery?"

That was what I was there for, so I said, "Sure," and turned to head for the OR.

"Not that way," he said. "Come with me."

Mystified, I followed him to the parking lot and climbed into his shiny Cadillac. I knew that to supplement his medical career, he owned a used car lot, "Doc's Clean Cars," and a tattered little roadside amusement park. "Where are we..." I started, but he held up a finger. "Just wait. You'll see."

We drove across town to a dilapidated hospital that catered to the Hispanic population of Tampa. Pulling around to the back, he extracted a key to a service door and led me up a dingy stairway to the second-floor surgery suite. Inside the first room was a middle-aged woman, already under anesthesia, her chest bare.

We changed into surgical scrubs. "Ever done a breast implant?" X asked. I shook my head, getting an increasingly bad feeling about this whole process.

"Nothing to it," he said. "Just follow my lead. You do one side, I'll do the other."

It became obvious that this whole enterprise was off the books. Doctor X would get his cash up front, do a surgery that he wasn't certified to do, and vanish into the Florida haze.

I didn't want any part of this, but at the same time I felt an obligation to this unknown woman lying unconscious on the table in front of us. Doctor X was not known as the best surgeon in Tampa. Even at my level of relative inexperience, I thought I could at least prevent a catastrophe. I swallowed hard and did my side of the breast implant, while Doctor X joked with the person giving the anesthesia. I didn't know if he was an actual anesthesiologist or even if he was a doctor, and I thought it best not to ask.

We finished. My side looked better. We changed and slipped down the back stairs to the Caddy and drove back to Tampa General. During the ride he peeled off a hundred-dollar bill from a wad he carried in his front pocket and wordlessly passed it over to me. I declined as politely as I could, my disgust rising at being tricked into being an accessory to this fraud.

I asked around discretely if anyone else knew about this activity. It seems most of the staff did know, but since Doctor X was connected, nobody wanted to rock the boat. I thought about making a stink, but as a first-year surgery resident I had about as much clout as the janitor. I never worked with him again.

———

As my year in Tampa drew to a close I knew I wanted to be a surgeon, but what flavor of surgeon would that be? Like many life-altering events, I drifted into the decision without a lot of thought.

My family is filled with doctors going back to my aforementioned horse-and-buggy great-grandfather. My grandfather and father were ear, nose, and throat (ENT) specialists. It seemed like interesting work. Hey, why not?

So for the next three years I learned the craft of head and neck surgery in a residency program in my home town of Indianapolis. Money was still tight, so I supplemented my residency salary by moonlighting in an emergency room. It was good real-world experience, as I was the only doctor there.

One especially hectic night I got a call from my wife. She was on the way to the hospital to deliver my second daughter. I was heartsick, but I was up to my ass in alligators. Since I was the lone doctor on duty I couldn't leave to be with her. Karen was born while I was delivering someone else's baby.

As doctors progress in their specialty training they're encouraged to take more responsibility in decision making. That's generally a good thing, as we'll be turned loose on an unsuspecting public soon and then we'll *have* to make our own decisions.

Senior surgeons will "staff" younger residents on cases. It's very much like the driving instructor sitting next to you, ready to punch the brakes or snatch the wheel if disaster is imminent. But you're doing the driving.

Such was the situation when Ron Hamaker, a nationally known ENT cancer surgeon, staffed me on a case. It was a difficult neck surgery, removing a tumor from the carotid artery.

By this time I was confident in my surgical skills. With some sweat and anxiety I got the job done. Ron, acting as my assistant, was uncharacteristically silent throughout the operation.

In the locker room afterward I noticed large circles on the armpits of his scrubs. "You okay?" I said.

"Where did you learn to use dissecting scissors like that?" he said.

"I don't know, probably doing nasal surgery. I like to dissect that way. Why?"

"Scared the living shit outta me," he said. "The carotid artery ain't the nose, Dorothy."

"But it went fine," I protested. "If you thought I shouldn't be doing it that way, why didn't you say something?"

"Your case," he said simply. He put a tired hand on my shoulder. "Bill, you and I are friends, so don't take this the wrong way. Never confuse luck with good technique. I was all set to have to graft a new carotid artery in there. I was your safety net. You're a good surgeon, but not good enough to start barnstorming."

It was a pivotal moment. I realized a couple of important things. First, and probably foremost, was that I wasn't ever going to be so good that I didn't need to constantly question what I was doing and how I was doing it. Second, always have a Plan B when the carefully considered Plan A goes down the toilet.

Suitably chastened, I spent the next thirty years as an otologist, an ear doctor. I rebuilt eardrums and reassembled the tiny bones that carry sound to the inner ear. Remember the hammer, anvil, and stirrup from biology class? That was me. I took out tumors where the hearing nerve hooks into the brain. I fixed dizzy patients.

Like many other stories of marrying too young and concentrating on a career, my wife and I grew apart and eventually divorced. It was not a pleasant experience, but the process convinced me that I'd divorced the right person.

I filled up the marital void with other pursuits. Got my private pilot's license. A friend who ran a Tae Kwon Do school convinced me to enroll. After fifteen years I accumulated three black belts and instructor's certificates in TKD and Aikido.

A technician buddy introduced me to computers by running a Lunar Lander game on a CT scanner during down time. I was hooked. I taught myself to program the beasts and ended up forming a company writing computer games.

Remember Dungeons and Dragons? We were the first to put it on a microcomputer. This was back in the days when a hard disc drive cost twenty grand and needed a hand truck to move it. My first storage device was a J.C. Penny tape recorder. We shoehorned our programs into 16K of memory, a thousand times less than the smallest cellphone has today. Still, we did such a good job that the folks that created the D&D board game sued us. Recognition of a sort.

I dated for years, but was gun-shy of commitment. I remodeled a small house in Indianapolis and indulged by installing a hot tub. Word got around surgery that Dr. Wright had a hot tub, a novelty in those days. The nurses kept teasing me about when I would have a hot tub party. Finally I said, "Great. You're all invited. Friday at seven."

Panic set in. Nobody actually wanted to come and sit in a hot tub at a doctor's house, but I'd called their bluff. Finally three of the nurses who felt guiltiest about fomenting the whole project agreed to come.

At the appointed hour, they appeared. I was a big stereo buff at the time. One nurse, a gorgeous redhead named Mollie, took one look at my record collection and practically fell on it, emoting about this and that classical recording. I thought, "Right. An operating room nurse who's a nut about classical music." Such an obvious ploy.

Of course, it turned out that Mollie *was* a nut about classical music, but couldn't afford to buy recordings on her salary. She knew more about the music, composers and history than anyone I'd ever met, certainly a lot more than I knew. We started to date.

She was divorced as well. What followed was ten years of one of us wanting to get married while the other held back. Then we'd switch roles, but never could get on the same page. Finally she got disgusted with me and got engaged to someone else. I was devastated. There was only one thing to do.

A couple of buddies and I got cigars and a bottle of Grand Marnier. We sat on the patio and plotted how I could win Mollie back from the brink of disaster. It was foolproof. I bought the engagement ring, tickets to Paris, corsage, Dom Perignon. I arranged for her to be off work and to have her two kids looked after during the honeymoon. All set.

I scheduled a late surgery when she would be working in the OR. I pleaded with her to come over after the case and she reluctantly agreed. When she arrived I had the music, the lights, the dinner all ready. I was charming. I proposed. She turned me down.

The story has an eventual happy ending. We've now been married for twenty-three years, and although I can't speak for her, it's the best thing that's ever happened to me.

The practice of otology was interesting and fun for a long time, but eventually the financial drain of managed care and the monotony of seeing the same things over and over again finally got to me. After almost thirty years of practice, I retired.

Retirement. I hated it. Mollie hated it more. I visited our kids in Colorado Springs and made some calls. An otologist friend asked if I'd be interested in running one of his two offices. I jumped.

After moving to Colorado Springs, I found the same burn-out with otology that I'd had back in Indiana. I needed something different.

I looked online for jobs. The Colorado Department of Corrections was looking for physicians. I applied. They were desperate. I was hired. A new career.

ELEVEN

GETTING UP TO SPEED

Throughout my career, I was never able to remember the generic names for drugs. The pill the drug company markets as Flub is actually acmerubinotersinosumab. Now which one sticks in your mind? Unfortunately for me, drug formularies and scientific articles use the generic names for medications so as not to show any bias. Bummer.

As an ear surgeon it didn't make a lot of difference. I had only a handful of drugs that I used on a regular basis, and I had pre-printed prescriptions. In my new career as a general practitioner I now supposedly knew *all* the drugs ever manufactured along with their interactions and side effects. And don't forget all the herbal stuff, nutritional supplements, and other over-the-counter medications.

How could I possibly pull off this feat of encyclopedic pharmaceutical legerdemain? In the old days we had a book called the PDR, the *Physician's Desk Reference*. The last one I got had nearly four thousand pages of really tiny type on really thin paper and weighed in like an unabridged dictionary. And that didn't include the Supplement.

You had to be dedicated, desperate, or both to break out the PDR, especially in front of a patient. So now that the responsibility for intimate knowledge of all the drugs in the Free World rested on my shoulders, what could I do? Fake it. Like the magicians, it's all smoke and mirrors.

With my trusty internet connection, I could look up Flub and find the jaw-breaking generic name that I had to use. Not only could I find all the information anyone could ever want about Flub, but also drugs that might be confused with it like Frac or Blub or acmerubinotersinosustatin.

Likewise, I quickly got in the habit of checking the latest and greatest on the diseases I was seeing. This was terrific. Senility was no longer a factor. I could look it up!

In my former life as a specialist I had a bias against treatment guidelines. I often disagreed with them through a combination of experience and prejudice. Most specialists resented the "cookbook medicine" that these guidelines engendered.

Adding injury to insult, these guidelines frequently found their way into required standards of care by third party payers like insurance companies or Medicare. If you didn't treat patients according to the guidelines, you didn't get paid. This is what's known as an incentive.

My stance changed as soon as I became a general practitioner. Since I was now supposed to know everything about everything, I welcomed a little help from the sidelines.

If a patient with ulcerative colitis came dragging into my clinic like Marley's ghost on Christmas Eve, it was a great comfort to us both that I could look up the guidelines on how to manage it. The guidelines, however, did not always take into account the realities of CDOC.

In the real world when you visit your doctor you expect to be offered the latest and best treatments for what ails you. At CDOC though, we're on a budget. This means that while the $15,000 per dose drug may be the Cadillac of treatments available today, we're still driving the Chevy.

It's not that the Chevy won't get you where you want to go. It just may take longer, or have more side effects that need to be managed, or be somewhat less effective. But it's cheaper. Usually a lot cheaper.

Now that's a good thing as long as the Chevy makes it to the top of the hill. This not only saves CDOC money along with the grateful taxpayers of Colorado, but also makes it more likely that the inmates will continue the medication if and when they finally hit the streets and have to foot the bills themselves.

If I needed a medication that wasn't on the approved list, I'd drop a line to my good friends on the Non-Formulary Committee (NFC). That's what I did when Fernando Gossman needed a new blood pressure medication. I sent a request detailing what I'd tried, why it hadn't worked, what the literature said should be done next. Sounds simple, right?

The response stumbled back: "Request denied. What kind of exercise program is Offender Gossman on?"

It's true that exercise has an effect on blood pressure, but since Gossman wasn't on the CSP volleyball team, it's kind of beside the point.

I dutifully faxed back with the same information in duplicate including a notation that Mr. Gossman didn't do a lot of exercise. Thanks for asking.

The request wound its ping-pong path to the NFC and back. "Request denied. No indication for this medication. Suggest HCTZ."

He'd already been on HCTZ and several others of its ilk. Gossman's blood pressure wasn't the only one on the rise. I shot back with all the original information along with a terse comment that he'd already failed this medication. I also might have mentioned that if the NFC thought that they had the inside track on how to solve this hypertension problem, they were welcome to come to CSP and take over Gossman's care. Otherwise please just honor the request of the doctor who is actually responsible for this guy and give me the damn pill. If I wanted a consultation, I'd have asked for it.

My frankness produced neither fruit nor blood pressure pills. "Request denied. Suggest you consult the Chief Medical Officer on this issue."

In words from Seinfeld, "No soup for you!"

Since you couldn't just wander into a supermax prison and browse around, families of CSP staff wondered what goes on where their spouses worked. There's an app for that: Family Night at the Prison.

After I'd been at CSP for about a year, the Warden decided that he'd invite the families of staff at CSP to tour the facilities. Just like other visitors, family members had to submit an application and go through an intel screening. They confirmed I hadn't married a thug or at least a wanted thug. Then it was time for the Big Night.

On the designated evening my wife, Mollie, met me at the Visitor's Center located outside the main prison guardhouse. We crowded into buses with a surprisingly large number of fellow tourists and headed to the CSP front gate. We got the standard lecture—no cell phones, no tobacco, no feeding the animals. Then the gate opened, and we all bustled into the main lobby.

After the security screens, we clustered in groups of ten in front of the sally port. I regarded the maw with the contempt of familiarity, but I could see the pucker factor kicking in all around. Remembering my first asthmatic trip into the port, I led my group into the lock with a mixture of empathy and smug superiority.

We entered the main corridors next to Master Control. Mollie was the first to speak. "It's clean!"

As an addict of true crime shows, she had visions of third-world prisons where rats and roaches outnumbered the prisoners by several orders of magnitude. Here at CSP, inmates from lower security prisons have nothing to do but empty, polish, disinfect, shine and scrub all day.

Our group of ten toured the main floor and then crammed into a tiny elevator to go up to a housing pod. The door closed. The elevator jerked. Stuck.

I had never been stuck in an elevator of any description, let alone with ten people packed like sardines in a minuscule cabinet deep in the bowels of a supermax prison. Deodorants failed. I'd like to say we all handled it well, but despite telling nervous jokes and singing a few camp songs, things were getting a little tense by the time the mechanics pried the doors open. We took the stairs for the rest of the visit.

Touring the housing pods was a lot like a trip to the zoo. The visitors stayed in groups and timidly peered into the units like viewing cages of dangerous predators, which, of course, they were. The inmates behaved well, as I'm sure they had been encouraged to do by the Warden. We finally retreated to the buses and a good time was had by all.

My wife said that she felt much better about my working at CSP after seeing the place for herself. I imagine with the public image of prisons on TV for comparison, that most of the families felt the same way. I hadn't given it much thought after the initial adjustment. I'm safer at CSP than I am at Walmart.

———

O utcast to the basement like the medical clinic, Intake is where prisoners go when they first arrive at CSP or when they've been naughty.

Assault a staff member? Refuse to cuff up? Break a sprinkler head and flood the pod? You're off to Intake.

Intake is a relatively small area with a horseshoe of cells around a central desk complex. Some of the cells have Lexan walls so the inmate can be constantly observed, while others have more conventional cells with tiny windows.

Going to Intake is like time-out for misbehavior. The inmate may be stripped to his boxer shorts and shackled while a video camera continuously records his actions. Mental health emergencies or violent inmates on special controls frequently require this. Special controls are any kind of restraint other than the usual handcuffs, belly chain, and foot shackles.

For some this means four-point restraints in a mini-reclining canvas chair on wheels. If you put on a straightjacket and wedge yourself into a toilet bowl, you'll get the idea. We have to be sure they don't strangle themselves in the restraint jacket. It's happened.

The officers watch while the inmate cools off, later to be returned to the housing pod with whatever privilege restriction is appropriate for the offense.

When I get called to intake, it's almost always something I'd rather avoid. Often the inmate in question is still mad as hell, uncooperative, and insulting. Frequently he still carries the lingering aroma of OC spray. OC, short for oleoresin capsicum, is also known as pepper spray.

It smells like the inside of a skunk and makes your eyes water like a bucket of onion juice.

My job was usually to do a visual inspection through the window for obvious injuries after a forced cell extraction and to determine if he needed any urgent medical care.

They rarely did. Aside from occasional abrasions from the inmate fighting the cuffs, injuries were uncommon. It's pretty amazing when you imagine the situation a short time earlier, with an enraged psychopath doing something he's not allowed to do in his cell. If the OC spray doesn't persuade him, the SORT team has to go in. Envision the NFL's Greatest Tackles highlight film played out in a broom closet. And yet there's seldom an injury.

When I did have to intervene, it was usually because the inmate had been cutting himself, and the wound is so severe that I can't let it go. Try sewing up a furious convict who spends all his waking hours working out. It's not as much fun as it sounds.

TWELVE

SORT AND HSAs

The Special Operations Response Team, or SORT, is made up of a
cadre of black-uniformed no-nonsense security personnel with
attitude. The SORT team are the guys who do "forced cell extractions"
when an inmate is having a bad day.

After the pod staff gives the angry miscreant plenty of opportunity
to shape up, the mental health folks might have a turn. But things being what they are at CSP, often SORT has to get him out of his cell and
escort him to Intake.

The SORT team consists of six officers dressed in black padded suits
and helmets. We're talking serious bulk here, like a ninja bomb disposal
unit. You could take baseball bats to these guys and they'd never feel it.

Each member of the team is responsible for a specific body part of
the offender. As they prepare in the ready room they count off: "I've got
the left arm." "I've got the right leg." When they open the cell door and
rush in, the poor bastard hasn't a prayer. It's like getting tackled by five
linebackers at once. One member of the team stays back and videotapes
the whole proceeding for the lawyers.

It might seem like this is overkill, but it produces much less opportunity for injury on either side. The inmate, if he gets a punch in at
all, might as well hit an onrushing mattress. The SORT members have

control so fast that there's not much in the way of a struggle where the inmate can get hurt. Usually there's not more than a scuff or two.

Before SORT rushes into the cell, they'll first use OC spray. They open the tray slot and insert a hose connected to a fire-extinguisher sized canister of OC. Normally a good snootful will incapacitate the inmate with coughing, runny nose, closed watering eyes, and difficulty breathing. But it doesn't work on everyone. I've seen some extractions where they've filled the cell with OC three times and still the offender wouldn't give up.

OC stinks up the place something fierce. Before the officers spray OC into an offender's cell, they have to clear anyone with asthma or chronic lung disease out of the pod. The potential use of OC also tends to decrease the number of onlookers. Water won't even wash it off and it's terrible cologne.

We had a pugilist at CSP in the days before they used OC spray. A huge inmate who just loved to fight, he'd purposely provoke the forced-cell team and slug it out until they finally subdued him.

Once, the first man through the door slipped and fell in front of the inmate. The officers behind couldn't get past their comrade, but the inmate didn't attack. He picked the fallen man off the floor, set him on his feet and asked if he was okay. When he got an affirmative answer from the shaken officer, the inmate motioned to the group at the door and said, "OK, let's start again."

When they started using OC spray on forced-cell situations, this particular inmate gave up and never caused trouble again. "No fun with the gas," he said.

Blair, my first Health Services Administrator (HSA), was a nurse with thirty years in the trenches. She was a stickler for rules and regulations, but knew what worked and how to get things done. When first practicing medicine in a prison setting, I'd often get caught by an inmate's simple request for a minor accommodation. I remember one exchange in particular, when she advised me to not grant a request for a lower tier.

I asked, "What's the big deal? Andolfo's got a bad knee. Why can't I give him a lower tier restriction?"

"You can," Blair said.

"I can? I just thought you said I couldn't do that."

"No. I said you shouldn't do that."

"Because..."

"How many kites do you want to get next week requesting a lower tier restriction because of knee pain? Or back pain? Or shoulder pain?"

"But—"

"You gave it to Andolfo. Why can't I have it?"

"Oh."

Blair was all about the practical application of medicine in this weird setting. She respected the knowledge and initiative that her medical crew brought to the table and suggested the best way to get results. She was more like a mentor than a supervisor. I really liked working with her.

So, of course, Blair retired.

For a few months the medical unit existed in a delicious unsupervised limbo. We kept doing the jobs we'd been taught to do, and everything was hunky peachy.

Then we got a new HSA, Herman, a social worker. As Seinfeld would say, "Not that there's anything wrong with that." The social services perform the vital and often thankless task of interfacing between the chaos inside a prison and the chaos without. I'm sure many social workers have the administrative acumen to bridge the gap and run a medical clinic. We just didn't happen to get one of those.

Herman showed his enthusiasm for his new post with a lot of "I appreciate all you do!" and "Great to have you on the team!" This may have worked well in the world of social work, but it apparently also gave him the impression that he knew how to run a medical practice.

Herman, God love him, wanted everyone to like him. I guess it goes with the social work ethic. At first I just kept out of his way, as it was painfully obvious he had no clue what medicine was all about. This proved to be impossible when he began to insist that certain inmates be immediately seen and treated. Why? Because they said they wanted to be seen right away. Everything became an emergency.

Inmates may be dumb, but they aren't stupid. Word got around quickly that the way to get to the front of the line was to bypass the doctor and complain directly to the HSA. Grandmothers joined in, calling Herman to demand their darlings be treated immediately for whatever supposed illness they had. Herman obliged.

I pulled rank and pointed out as diplomatically as I could that while he might technically be my supervisor, he was a social worker and I was a medical doctor. I should decide who got an appointment and who didn't. That didn't fly either.

The next day I arrived at the clinic to find a schedule overflowing with kites for trivial and nonsensical complaints. The nurses looked at the list in amazement. Why are we seeing all these bozos? Because Herman says so. It makes his numbers look good.

A call from Herman was also waiting for me. An inmate had declared a medical emergency, and I would see him right now! What exactly was this emergency? He didn't know, but I would see this inmate immediately!!

So the clinic stopped. The folks with diabetes and high blood pressure and chest pain just had to get rescheduled. The escorts brought the inmate over to see about his medical emergency. What is it? He had a stuffy nose last night. All better now.

Here's a tip for all the felons reading this book: If you don't like something, have your mom call. It's amazing how many hardened criminals at CSP go crying to their mothers about whatever it is they happen to want at the moment. Mom calls the lawsuit-shy prison administrators with a tale of abuse. Bingo! Junior is bumped to the front of the line. Feeling neglected? Forget calling your attorney. Call Mom.

In an effort to create more time for clinic, Herman instituted a policy of no lunch breaks for anyone. I called Herman to protest this latest indignity, but couldn't get through. He was out to lunch.

Thirteen

The Prisoners Take Charge

C ivil rights for prisoners sounds like a good thing. For me, it was a pain in the ass.

The Eighth Amendment bars the use of "cruel and unusual" punishment, although what that represents was left up in the air. In 1848 the Supreme Court noted that such punishments would include "drawing and quartering, emboweling alive, beheading, public dissecting, and burning alive." Rats. Took away some of my favorites.

In modern penology, anything that violates a person's dignity can be considered cruel and unusual. Since many of the CSP inmates have marginal dignity to begin with, this leaves a lot of room for interpretation.

I got all sorts of kites and grievances under protestations of inhumane treatment. The common denominator was the inmate's unshakable belief that he was "entitled."

"My mattress isn't thick enough," (it was).

"I'm allergic to fish," (he wasn't).

"I need snacks," (he didn't).

"I need a lower bunk, elevator pass, double cuffs, a vacation in the Bahamas," (please).

When Angelo Washington came to the clinic, I knew things weren't going to go well as this was his third visit for the same issue. Although cuffed to a belly chain, Angelo had a batch of papers clutched in both hands. He started off with an attitude.

"You got to give me two mattresses. My back is killin' me. It's inhumane. Cruel and unusual."

"Actually, Mr. Washington, I don't need to do anything except keep you alive. Everything else is on the a la carte menu."

"Right here it says," he continued, rustling the papers in my direction, "you got to give me the right stuff for my back."

"You've got the right stuff. You've got a mattress and you can get pain medicine off the canteen."

He shook the papers emphatically. "Bullshit. My chiropractor right here says I need a thick mattress. You denying me my rights."

"You have the right to one mattress like everybody else."

"You don't know shit. My chiropractor says—"

"Do you see your chiropractor here?"

"No. I got it right here, what he said. You discriminating..."

That was it. The "D" word. I motioned to the COs that the interview was over. "I don't give a rip what your chiropractor said. He's not here. I am. You're in prison, not a spa. You can buy yourself a Temper-Pedic when you get out."

I'm not a member of the NRA or the ACLU, but sometimes I had to step outside of my professional persona and smell the coffee. I consistently witnessed a boatload of petty complaints and niggling grievances from hateful people who continually demanded their "right" to this or that. I often felt that the ideal of civil rights had been hijacked and held at gunpoint by a bunch of grandstanding terrorists.

Still, if you behave like the animals, you are one. One of the mottos of my first warden at CSP was, "People are sent to prison *as* punishment, not *for* punishment." He was right. It's not up to me or anyone else at CSP to make a prisoner's life more miserable. He's got enough of that already.

It was not my purview to deny an inmate the best medical treatment I could provide just because I didn't like what he did to get here. My wife is an inveterate watcher of true crime shows. When I first took this job, she was always asking what lurid crimes my patients had committed.

She couldn't understand when I told her I didn't know, and that I didn't want to know. If someone was a forger, a burglar, a rapist, a child molester, or a murderer would I treat him differently? Maybe I would. So unless it bears on my medical treatment, I don't want to know. Ignorance is bliss.

———

The Supreme Court ruled that state and federal prison systems and their administrators could be held personally liable for damages when the health and welfare of inmates was treated with "deliberate indifference." Whoops!

The inmates took this as a guarantee to get whatever they happened to want. If I didn't give an inmate the pain medicine he wanted, suddenly I was "deliberately indifferent" to his needs and civil rights.

Of course that's not what "deliberately indifferent" means at all. It's supposed to mean that if an inmate has a significant medical problem, and I decide to ignore it out of laziness or meanness or whatever, then I'm "deliberately indifferent" to his problem. That's what it's supposed to mean.

A day seldom passed without a kite or grievance from an inmate with "deliberate indifference" in quotes and underlined to show how legally savvy he was. The threat was I'd better get my act together and give him his (fill in the blank), or I'd be hearing from his attorney. Here's one from Ralph Arbury, an arsonist from New Mexico who fell off a roof fleeing police, tearing a ligament in his knee:

"My knee's in TERRIFIC pain for months while you ignore my SERIOUS MEDICAL ISSUES. I need surgery immediately to fix this but I get NOTHING from medical. All you care about is saving a buck and are being DELIBERATELY INDIFFERENT to my medical needs. This is my LAST REQUEST before I start LEGAL ACTION!!"

Well, I guess he told me. I wasn't so much indifferent to Arbury's problem as terminally annoyed. He'd screwed up his knee nearly ten years ago, and it hadn't seemed to slow down his crime career. His injury might have ended his aspirations as a professional athlete, but since he stood only 5"4", the NBA seemed like a stretch. His mobility needs at CSP consisted of getting his ass out of his bunk and making it to the door to get his food. He could fall down and still cover the distance.

Inmates who wanted a free surgery as well as a change of scenery sent messages like this. The threat of lawsuits was mostly smoke, but sometimes they'd go to the mat and file. These were a nuisance to CDOC, but fortunately nobody gave these complaints much credence except the Colorado Board of Medical Examiners. Apparently great advocates for the rights of felons, the Board always wanted an exhaustive written report from me personally detailing why Arbury or whoever was on deck at the moment wasn't getting the compassionate care he obviously deserved. This from a group of self-important donut-eaters who didn't have clue one about what goes on inside a prison. Don't get me started.

It's true that health care has been the stepchild of the prison system since time began. The people who view prisons as only punishment argue strenuously that we should make them as uncomfortable as possible. No coddling those bastards. Kill a few if you can.

The other side of the social spectrum wants everyone to get along. Prisoners are just misunderstood, like the song in *West Side Story*. They deserve all the rights and privileges everyone else enjoys, including the best medical care available. Just don't try to raise taxes to pay for it.

In the old days, prisoners were their own doctors. With the advent of inmate labor, convicts became the unofficial nurses and doctors in prison facilities nationally. It was common for inmates to assist with surgeries performed inside the prison walls. No longer. Take two aspirin and call me in ten years doesn't fly anymore.

Most of us don't think of prison inmates as having health problems. On the TV shows prisoners are steroid-pumped hulks bench-pressing three hundred pounds with a pinkie.

That's true for lots of them. But we've also got Alzheimer's and AIDS patients, wheelchair-bound paraplegics, hypertensives, cancer victims and guys with epilepsy. Remember Richard Kimball's one-armed man in *The Fugitive* series? He's here too.

———

It's an old prison maxim that when you do your time, your whole family does it with you. The loss of contact with friends and family is part of the deal when you're incarcerated, but not much thought is given to the separation experienced by those on the outside. Wives without husbands, children without a father. Loss of income. All are obvious but often overlooked penalties paid by the family left behind.

Currently, there are more than two million adults in prison or jail in the United States. The majority of both men and women in prison are parents of children under the age of eighteen.

As much as I hate statistics, a few help here with perspective. It's estimated that 1.7 million American children have a father in prison and 200,000 a mother. Sixty-five percent of women and 55% of men in Colorado prisons have a child under eighteen. A third of these men have more than one child.

Nationally, 75 percent of women in prison are mothers who have two or three children under the age of eighteen living with them prior to their arrest and imprisonment. Eighty-five percent of the children who have a mother in prison are under the age of ten. Six percent of women enter prison pregnant.

So what happens to these kids? Not surprisingly, they are much more likely to have academic and behavior problems in school. They are more likely to be into drugs and delinquency. Half of female juveniles and 25 percent of male juveniles in detention have had a parent in prison at some time in their lives. Children who have a mother in prison are six times more likely to be incarcerated in their lifetime than children who live in poverty but who don't have a mother in prison.

These are depressing statistics that point out the impact of the loss of a parent on the children left behind. There are all sorts of arguments about the effect of a criminally-inclined parent on their children when they are present in the home, but there's no denying that having dad or mom in prison is a big minus on a child's future prospects.

Organizations like Big Brothers and Big Sisters attempt to compensate and correct this deficit, but they can't be fulltime like a parent. Foster homes and staying with relatives are something of a crapshoot. Adoption is an option for some, but carries its own set of problems.

What about the spouse left outside? Somebody's got to bring home the bacon, and that means mom or dad is out at a job instead of being home with the kids. Incarceration of a spouse isolates the one left outside and brands him or her with the stigma of the imprisonment. There is an 85 percent divorce rate among couples where one spouse is imprisoned for a year or more; 80 percent for incarcerated men and almost 100 percent for women.

I rarely have contact with the families of the men I'm seeing, but I never forget that my inmate patients usually have ties to outside family and friends. From a medical perspective there's not much I can do. When a previously controlled diabetic starts having sugar problems or a hypertensive goes through the roof, trouble with the outside world is often involved. I need to consider these influences in my therapy. Bringing in the mental health folks to help with blood pressure might seem a little odd, but it may work wonders.

Instead of being a source of support, families often show themselves to be part of the problem. Bob Amster is a three-time loser car thief. A recent call from his mom to the CSP nursing administrator while I was in her office illustrates:

"You're discriminating against my boy. He didn't do nothing wrong. He should be on that seizure medicine."

"Your son was taken off of the medication because he was found with a cache of thirty pills in his cell, and he was selling them."

"But he needs that medicine!"

"He doesn't need it if he doesn't take it. Do you understand he was pretending to take the pills, but instead he was keeping them out and then selling them?"

"Not his fault."

"Not his fault? Whose fault is it?"

"Your fault. You supposed to make sure he taking the pills."

"We try to do that, but he's the one who's supposed to take them. Don't you understand he was stealing the medicine to sell?"

"Like he's not supposed to do that."

"No. He's not supposed to do that. He knows that. That's why he was hiding the pills."

"If he show you the pills, you just take them away."

"That's right. He's not supposed to keep them. He's supposed to take them when we bring them."

"But you not bringing them anymore. That be your fault."

And so it goes. Thanks, Mom for all you do...and did.

Holding down an honest job is, strangely enough, one of the privileges inmates seek. While the best they can do in the supermax is mopping the floor, less restrictive prisons offer real opportunities.

Colorado prisons are big on vocational rehabilitation. All the programs of Colorado Correctional Industries (CCI) pay for themselves and teach skills the inmates can use on the outside when they parole.

CCI has an internal benefit to the prisons. Inmates often come in with no work ethic, no conscience, and no basic educational skills. They're motivated to get into the CCI programs because they pay much better than sitting in a cell. Pay is tied to productivity and level of responsibility. Teamwork pays off in cash as well as in better socialization. Many of the inmates have never been in any kind of cooperative work environment.

CCI runs an incredible number of operations, from breaking wild mustangs to making canoes and fly rods. Inmates tend the grapes for the Holy Cross Abbey winery and run a huge organic dairy operation.

I took a tour of the tilapia farm. I had to duck under pipes to enter the low building on land near the Arkansas River. Colorado doesn't have much humidity, but the interior of the farm building fogged up my glasses instantly.

Huge stainless steel troughs about four feet deep and wide stretched to the end of the building. Plastic pipes snaked along the sides and overhead. Pressure valves studded the walls. Brownish water bubbled with aeration. Not much happening here. Kind of tranquil.

"Want to see them feed?" asked an inmate worker. As he approached one of the tanks with a white plastic bucket, fish began to break the surface. "They know what it means when I come with the bucket," he said.

He scattered a handful of brown pellets, and the water exploded with six-inch fish snapping up the food. It looked like a National Geographic special of piranhas eating a cow. The water boiled for about fifteen seconds then became placid once more.

"Jesus! You don't want to get too close to that," I said.

"Oh, they're not bad, but I'd probably keep my hand away," he said.

I toured greenhouses with blooms erupting from every corner. The new shrimp-raising house was being rigged with pipes. Cattle and goat farms covered a portion of the prison land behind a mesa.

"It's been years since we've had to buy any stock," said my guide, gesturing to the herds. "Now we sell excess stock off to other farmers. Like goat cheese?"

Remembering my last prison lunch, I declined.

I got acquainted with their K-9 adoption program when our dog died of cancer. My wife found Annie, a sort of poodle/schnauzer mix on the CCI website. All the dogs in the program are rescued from their own death row situations. Each one is paired with an inmate who has qualified for the training program. Dog and new master spend the next six weeks socializing and learning basic obedience commands.

We drove to the Women's Prison in Cañon City just before Christmas to pick up Annie. The program coordinator told us that there was another dog whose potential owner had backed out at the last moment. If nobody took him, it was back to the pound. He had been rescued along with Annie from a dumpster in Pueblo. Would we be interested?

So now we've got Annie, a black ball of curls, and Harry, a white terrier/something mix. The chaos twins. They were both so excited and nervous on the trip home they threw up, peed and pooped all over the car. Welcome to civilian life.

FOURTEEN

ANNUAL REFRESHER TRAINING AND OTHER TIME WASTERS

I f there's one thing CDOC is big on, it's training. Some classes are what you might expect, like proficiency in the use of firearms, forced cell entry, and escape procedures. These might be fun, so I don't qualify for any of them.

Annual CPR training is available for everyone, as are refresher courses on gang activity and the various dodges that criminals use. Some are more off the wall like, "What Color is your Personality?" and even one on how to be a hostage. Cool.

The one I dread most is the Annual Refresher Course (ARC), a two-day funfest packed with lectures about safety and administration. It's so boring that most staffers would rather go to work. The first lecture is entitled "Slips, Trips and Falls." I'll have to admit there was a lot of pertinent information. For instance, I learned:

- Oil is slippery
- Ice is slippery too
- You can trip over stuff
- If you trip, you might fall down
- Hot things can burn you
- Don't put a live wire in your mouth

Hot stuff. Then we got to play "Jeopardy" with Administrative Regulations (ARs) as the subjects. Which AR concerns the scope of services for gender identity disorders? Is it 700.12 or 700.14? The tension was damn near unbearable.

After a potty break we plowed right into PowerPoint Slide Hell. This was an unusual twist on the traditional PowerPoint presentation as there was an audio track, but no visuals. After wrestling with the computer and connections, we then got the flip side: visuals with no audio. Finally our lecturer just told us to read the slides and walked out of the room.

Our safety officer, nicknamed Code Red, once again reminded us about the vital importance of Materials Safety Data Sheets. I did pick up a valuable tip. Don't put paint stripper in your water bottle. Apparently someone actually did this and....

Even prison fires were covered. Arson does occur in prisons. Inmates set fires for suicides (ugh!), malicious destruction, escape schemes, shows of force, as well as the occasional accident.

Fires are more dangerous in a prison setting than in your average office building mainly because of difficult access. The fire department can't just pull up and start busting out windows and chopping holes in the roof.

In a fire the COs lead the way, evacuating inmates and opening a passage for firefighters. This is not a quick process, and inmate fire drills are out of the question. That's why we're sprinklered to the hilt. We haven't had any substantive fires at CSP to date, so the only use the sprinklers get is to flood the pods when inmates break them.

Fire is one reason why they make prisons out of non-combustible materials. No rugs, no curtains, no sofas. Concrete doesn't burn. Neither does steel furniture. I'm feeling pretty safe on that score. If Cañon City caught fire and burned to the ground, I'd never know it until I went out to my car.

Nonetheless, we got a lecture on the different types of fire extinguishers. A through F. I can't at the moment remember what they're for, but it's very important to use the right one on the right fire. That would be the one locked in master control two floors up.

The first section of the Annual Refresher Course ends with the reminder that we're all professionals. It comes right after the fifteen-minute review on which way to point the fire extinguisher.

Potentially the most helpful section of the ARC is the Pressure Point Control Techniques refresher course. Here we learned that if you push **Right Here** it hurts like hell. It's kind of like the Vulcan Death Grip. Supposedly this enables a ninety-pound secretary to bring an enraged 250-pound maniac to his knees in an instant. In theory.

I have severe doubts that in the heat of the moment the secretary would remember all these neat nerve pressure points. A good scream seems in order.

———◆———

One of the things I've had to get used to is not being a doctor anymore. I'm now a healthcare provider. I'll admit that I feel the loss of status, and it does rankle a bit.

Ever since Medicare came in, the bean counters have tried to lump physicians with all the rest of the physician's assistants, nurse practitioners, midwives, and Native American shamans so they can pay them less.

The truth is, physicians *are* different. I don't mean to sound exalted, but when you've fought your way through a couple of decades of specialized training and end up with the ultimate responsibility for other people's lives and health as well as supervising the other members of the healthcare team, you *are* different. Even the personal-injury lawyers know that.

But not CDOC. We're all the same. Providers. So we have provider meetings.

All the prisons have video conferencing capabilities, but everyone has to personally travel across the state to the jail in East Podunk so we can "become acquainted with other facilities." Hmm. Looks like another prison to me. Razor wire. Bars. Yep, it's a prison. Certainly glad I drove two hours to see this.

The fact that the meetings change nothing should come as no surprise to anyone who has worked in a bureaucracy. The meeting two months ago featured inmate obesity. The CDOC policy of encouraging a healthy diet and exercise wasn't working. We suspected that prisoners stuffing themselves with Twinkies and cupcakes while lying in their bunks all day had something to do with it. We thrashed the subject around for several hours, finally deciding that the solution was diet and exercise. Wow. Glad we got that settled. Now it's a two-hour drive back.

The theme of one meeting early in my tenure addressed how we could improve the CDOC computer system. We knew we couldn't begin to fix its arthritically slow performance, but had high hopes we could suggest some remedies for a multitude of petty annoyances.

I used to be a computer programmer, and have a pretty good idea of what's easy to fix and what's hard. In the meeting I enumerated a half dozen simple fixes that would remove a boatload of roadblocks in our daily computer work. Everyone enthusiastically agreed. Notes were taken. Assurances made. Result? Nada. Not a single change. That was four years ago.

Ripping away the cloak of collegiality, the real purpose of the provider meetings is to inform us of decisions administration has already made without consulting us. Saves the wear and tear of email. Some highlights of a recent meeting: (1) Nobody gets lunch (2) No matching in the retirement plan and (3) We'll be double-covering because of staff shortages. Except for that, it was pretty uplifting.

FIFTEEN

MONTEZ

Jesse Montez was a thief who became hemiplegic after an auto accident. He sued the state to get access to prison programs. After eleven years of class-action wrangling, the case was settled and Jesse got five thousand bucks. Of course, he was dead by then, but the lawyers made out okay. The Montez accommodation is supposed to ensure that inmates with disabilities have access to prison programs. That's the good part.

The bad part is the class-action lawyers just couldn't let this cash cow die. Now it was a matter of "ensuring compliance."

The class-action legal team hauled CDOC back to court to dictate in legally explicit language exactly who was disabled, how disabled they were and precisely what medical treatment and other accommodations they needed. In other words, the lawyers wanted to be doctors. Does anyone see a train wreck coming?

After eighteen years of legal thrashing, the product landed on my desk. Montez says that a medical provider (that would be me) will evaluate any poor slob who sends in a form for his claimed disability. One of my absolute favorites was a claim for a mobility disability.

On the face of it, this looked like a pretty straightforward item. I was supposed to determine if a guy locked down 23/7 in a cell the size of a walk-in closet was mobile enough to function. That should take about thirty seconds. But I forgot the lawyers were running the show.

I had to fill out the lawyer's physical examination forms (LPEF). Have you ever seen a *medical* physical exam form? It's a single page with room left over to do a crossword. But the LPEF? Eleven (count 'em) pages. In columns. With penetrating questions like "Does the inmate sit down to take off his socks?" and "Can the inmate lie down on the examination table?" Gee, I don't know. He probably just stands up in a corner at night.

After gathering the inmate's wish list for accommodations, doing the physical exam and entering the eleven pages of data into the computer, I'd blown an hour or so. Then I got to do the whole thing over again in two weeks. Same questions, same physical, same forms. Why? Because the judge said so, that's why. After all, who knows better how to evaluate a physical disability than a team of lawyers? It really makes you yearn for Guatemalan jails.

Ray Rawlins was a fairly typical Montez applicant. Ray could press two-fifty and was runner-up in the how-many-pushups-can-you-do marathon. Ray had a backache. He wanted double mattresses, an extra pillow, a lower tier and bunk, an excuse so he didn't have to do any jobs, and a bucket of painkillers. He found medical unsympathetic to his plight, so he filled out his Montez papers claiming he was disabled due to chronic back pain (excruciating).

The papers said Ray could claim to be disabled because of hearing, vision, diabetes, or mobility. He went for mobility.

His next stop was seeing me for a "mobility evaluation." You might think I'd check out how his chronic back pain was preventing him from being able to walk. Not so.

I took out my goniometer, a two-armed device for measuring angles, and proceeded to document the different angles of flexion and extension in his leg joints. I pulled out my tape and measured the circumference of his calves and thighs. I measured the density of hair on his legs. I checked his pulses. All of this vital data was duly recorded on the LPEF sheets. During all these machinations, Ray was growing increasingly restive.

"What about my mattress?"

"I'm not allowed to tell you anything about that. The lawyers will let you know."

Ray squirmed, presumably in excruciating pain. "My back hurts."

"Sorry to hear that. If you want something done about it, put a kite in to medical."

"What are you doing now?"

"I'm measuring the growth of hair on your lower legs."

"What's that got to do with my back?"

"Nothing, as far as I can tell."

"This is bullshit."

"Bingo."

After years of wrangling over the Big Three disabilities—mobility, hearing and vision—the lawyers snuck in diabetes. This is apparently to ensure that medical won't leave the exercise yard littered with comatose diabetics. I can't figure out why diabetes should be a disability. It's a disease that's treatable. If somebody with high blood pressure isn't disabled, why should a diabetic? Maybe it's a memorial to the original Jesse Montez, who was also a diabetic.

There's a final category of last resort for a Montez disability. Like most things legal, the attorneys insisted on an escape clause for anything they couldn't get the judge to expressly include—the dreaded "Other" category.

This category was created so that anyone could claim an ADA disability for anything at all. No need to be stumbling around blind, deaf, or crippled. Just claim you've got a bad case of "Other."

You might expect people to be reasonable about what's disabling, but, remember, this is prison. Hangnails, dry skin, boogers? Bring 'em on. Reasonableness gets left in the parking lot along with your MP3 player and cell phone.

Once, I had an inmate claim an "Other" disability because he wanted more electrical outlets in his cell. He only had two outlets and wanted to simultaneously plug in his radio, TV, fan, and CPAP machine.

Now, I couldn't just blow it off as a stupid request because a federal judge has ruled anything goes with the "Other" category. Each claim must be fully evaluated and documented. So I had to do an "evaluation" and fill out the bazillion Montez forms because this idiot felt he was electrically disabled. In my humble opinion, I don't get paid nearly enough, but this morning I don't think the Colorado taxpayers got their money's worth. Thanks, judge.

———

M ontez isn't the only time and money pit around. I recently finished the workup of a young inmate who escaped from the county jail by crawling out a ventilation shaft on an upper floor. He then proceeded to fall forty feet to the pavement, impaling himself on a steel fence post. Hey, it looked like a great plan on paper.

He sued the state for not preventing his escape and causing his subsequent injury. The defense was lucky he didn't have a hot cup of coffee with him, or the damages could have been enormous.

The impaling severed several nerves in his nether regions and required bringing the bowel out to the surface in an ileostomy. The surgeons couldn't put him back together at that time because of the nerve damage.

CDOC spent a small fortune over two years testing and monitoring the state of the nerves until it was determined that they had recovered enough to put the bowel back together again. Then CDOC refused to approve the surgery because they "don't reverse ileostomies." Maybe someone should have thought of that a couple of years ago. But I'm just hired help.

Sixteen

On Call and Emergencies

E ven dedicated physicians like me go home at night. That means somebody has to be on a rotation call for emergencies. Unfortunately, when you're on call, you're on call for every prison in the state. Although it made for an active evening, telephone medicine brought its own set of problems.

When I was in front of a live patient, especially a prison inmate, non-verbal cues were more important than what the guy was saying. Excruciating pain was suspect when the patient arrived laughing and joking with the COs. But I couldn't tell that on the phone. I had to depend on what a nurse, or sometimes a non-medical CO, was telling me.

Some things were straightforward. If a diabetic inmate celebrated Sadie Hawkins Day by eating three candy bars, no problem. Pour in the insulin.

Others choices were murky. I got a call about Shane Swire, a congenital liar and aficionado of road trips to the emergency room, who was complaining of crushing chest pain and shortness of breath. It was two in the morning. The EKG machine was out of paper. The vital signs were pretty normal. What to do?

I couldn't examine Swire (and he knew this). If I followed my gut and told them to put him back to bed, this might have been the one time he actually tried to die. Or I could have played it safe and spent a few grand of the state's money so Swire could get an ambulance ride and chat up the nurses in the ER.

A sharp nurse can make all the difference. If I had one of those on the phone, I'd ask "What do you think?"

Now traditionally, nurses are not supposed to think. Like soldiers, they're supposed to follow orders. It takes some of them aback when a physician asks for their opinion, but they're the ones seeing this guy lounging in the clinic in absolutely no distress at all. They're the ones who have seen Swire pull this charade a dozen times and know the difference between someone in trouble and someone who just wants a little diversion.

If I'm lucky enough to have one of these on the phone, Swire often gets put back to bed because I can trust the nurse's experienced eye. If I get one of the less experienced ones, Swire likely gets a ride.

Not surprisingly, telephone medicine had its weird moments. On one occasion, I got a nighttime call from a prison in Denver.

"Dr. Wright, we don't have a provider here and Mr. Spanner has just died. We need a physician to pronounce him."

"Is this unexpected?"

"No, he had very advanced liver cancer."

"And you want me to tell you if he's dead."

"Yes, sir."

"Okay. Put him on the phone."

"He can't come to the phone. He's dead."

"We'll see. Ask him if he'd like an injection of morphine."

"Ask him?"

"Sure."

"Uh, he doesn't seem to want any."

"Now ask him if he'd like extra snacks at bedtime."

"Umm. I don't think so."

"Let's see. Doesn't want phone calls. Doesn't want drugs. Doesn't want snacks. Okay, he's dead."

C DOC is a bureaucracy, no doubt about that. It's the worst part of the job as far as I'm concerned. Coming from private practice where I made my own decisions, I have trouble with other people telling me what to do and how to do it.

Regardless of the drawbacks, almost everyone says, "It's the easiest job I've ever had." Indeed, this is why many stay on. Nurses who are burned out by being required to do more and more in short-staffed hospitals, physician assistants being pressured to see extra patients in private practices, doctors fleeing higher overhead and lowering reimbursements, all are prime candidates for the cocoon of CDOC.

I chafe against the incursion of non-medical supervisors and pharmacists into medical decisions that are above their pay grade. The nonsense of bureaucratic regulation drives me nuts. I have to admit, though, it *is* the easiest job I've ever had.

To say that it's a tranquil pace is a gross understatement. Things move at glacial velocity in a prison. After all, nobody's going anywhere.

Also, we work for the government. This adds another layer of indolence. If the job got any more relaxed, I'd slip into a coma. After the pressures of private practice, it's easy to be seduced by the mañana mentality of CDOC. All we need is a margarita machine.

A t CSP our emergency room is little more than an area where we wring our hands while waiting for the 911 medics to arrive. Pretty much without exception, any drug that would actually help in an emergency isn't here because it's contraband. If an inmate from any of the CDOC prisons isn't sick enough to be in the hospital, but is too sick to be in a cell at his home prison, he lands in the infirmary at Colorado Territorial Correctional Facility across town.

Territorial opened for business as the original Colorado State Penitentiary in 1871. Although the fortress-like structure has modern parts tacked on, most of the original structure still stands. And who occupies the most ancient and decrepit part of the prison? Medical.

Because CDOC is chronically short-staffed, I sometimes get volunteered to work either the clinic or the infirmary at Territorial.

The infirmary consists of a huge central area with two-bed rooms lining opposite walls. At the far end, a separate area has a half dozen ad seg (administrative segregation) rooms where the bad boys and crazies go. The nurse's station takes up the remaining wall with windows facing out to the central area.

A sign on the nursing station door read, "Do Not Open Door With Key." Since the door was locked, it wasn't obvious how else to get in. I asked.

"Oh, they don't want you to pull on the key to open the door. Turn the key and pull the door open with the handle."

Seems simple enough until you've got a pile of charts in one hand and the key in the other. I elected to ignore the instructions and do what worked. I imagine I'll pull the lock out of the door before I'm done. I'm practicing being astonished and innocent.

The pressure is intense to get people out of the infirmary since it only has thirty-two beds. If it's full, the only choice is to ship inmates to Denver or keep them in a secure lockup at a hospital, both awkward and expensive choices.

I hate the infirmary. One of the most valuable assets a physician has is information about what happened before he showed up. This usually takes the form of a patient's history, but in a prison situation I can't count on getting any reliable information from the patient.

The medical team at Fremont Correctional Facility sent Kevin Ownby, a 52-year-old pedophile, to the emergency room because of chest pain. He was released back to prison via the Territorial infirmary.

"What happened at the ER?" I asked Carol, one of the infirmary nurses.

"Beats me," she said. "They don't send records to us."

I flipped through the chart. The only thing from the hospital stay was some boilerplate headed by, "Thank you for choosing St. Elsewhere for your medical needs."

"This is ridiculous. Get the ER doc on the phone."

A call to the emergency room revealed that the doctor who saw Ownby was off duty. No records would be available until the notes were dictated and transcribed in a few days. In the meantime Ownby sat propped up in an infirmary bed watching TV.

"So, Mr. Ownby, what did they have to say at the ER?"

"They gave me some blue pills."

"OK, but what did they say the pills were for?"

"I dunno. Musta been serious, 'cause they kept me there a long time."

"They didn't tell you what was wrong?"

"Something about arthritis or something. I couldn't understand it very well."

"Arthritis? You went there for chest pain."

"Oh, yeah, that too."

"That too, what?"

"I had some chest pain."

"We knew that before you went to the hospital."

"Yeah. Guess you were right."

If the patient is one of my guests at CSP, I've probably treated him before. I have something in the past to compare with the present situation. But the patients in the infirmary are mostly from other prisons and I haven't a clue about their previous behaviors. Maybe he's been sick for years. Maybe something radically changed recently. If someone is short of breath, it's helpful to know that he's been short of breath for the last ten years instead of just the last ten minutes.

I might find notes that my predecessors have put in the chart, but unless they're regulars in the infirmary, they're as clueless as I am about why this guy is lying here. This leaves the nurses.

A typical day might find me assigned to the infirmary to care for a couple dozen patients. I've never seen them before, have no idea why they're here, and have only the tiniest smidgeon of data about their conditions. If you've ever gone into an examination with the horrible realization that you've studied the wrong chapter, you know the feeling. On this particular day I gamely approached the first bed with nurse Carol in tow.

I leafed through piles of irrelevant paper in the patient's chart. "So, Carol, tell me about Mr. Schein."

"He's here for cancer."

"To get it?"

"No. They did surgery at St. Elsewhere."

"And the surgery was...?"

Carol called to her colleague in the nursing station. "Hey, Betty! You got anything about Schein's surgery?"

"Nope. Report should be here in a couple of days."

Carol turned back to me. "I think it was his pancreas."

"I think it was his liver," Betty called.

"Anyway, he's doing fine."

Just to cross-check I thought I'd ask the patient. "So how are you feeling, Mr. Schein?"

Eyes glazed, Schein wobbled his head away from the TV. "Great, Doc. Can I get some more of those pink pills? I forget what they call them. Something with a 'P' I think. Per...something. Percocet. That's it! Percocet. I'm really hurting."

"I thought you felt great."

Schein, drugged to the gills was slow to recover from his tactical blunder. "Well, yeah. I mean I feel good now, but I can feel it coming on again."

"It?"

"You know."

"I do."

Fortunately I have a surgical background, so I can usually tell if Schein is an impending catastrophe. However, since I'd never seen him before, I couldn't readily tell if he was getting better or not. I progressed to the next patient, Mr. Ebert, who had intercepted a bullet with his right calf.

I removed the dressing from his leg. "Looks pretty clean. Carol, how's it look compared to yesterday?"

"I was off yesterday."

"How about the last time you saw it? When was that?"

"I've been on the other side. I haven't seen it before."

"How about it, Mr. Ebert? Looking better?"

Ebert smiled up from a codeine-induced haze. "Looks good, Doc. Hey, can I get some more of those pink pills?"

Now I don't mean to imply that the inmates weren't getting the correct care. I just didn't know. So I made my best assessment and plunged ahead. It was a little like choosing which wire to cut defusing a bomb. Red or green? Maybe the white one. None of the above? Take your pick and pull out the snippers. I was the bomb squad.

A phenomenon unique to the infirmary was the two-bed rooms. It's amazing how symptoms ping-pong between the beds. It would make things a lot easier if I just treated each pair of patients for the same diseases. Douglas and Malik were roommates.

"So how are the bowels working today, Mr. Douglas?"

"I got piles, Doc," said Malik.

"I'll be with you in a minute, Mr. Malik. How about it, Mr. Douglas?"

"Pretty good, but my throat's a little sore."

Malik again. "I think I caught the same thing. My throat's raw. Can't hardly swallow."

"Hold on, Mr. Malik. Let's take a look, Mr. Douglas."

Douglas attempts further explanation with a tongue blade in his throat. "I byrthmnrugrth a unbrph"

"Don't talk. Just open."

Malik, unhampered by the tongue depressor, chimes in. "I got some of that too. I think I need one of those green things."

"Looks OK, Mr. Douglas. Just a little irritated from the anesthetic tube you had."

Malik, ever helpful again: "That tube's a bitch. I been sore for a week."

"Mr. Douglas had his appendix out. You're in here for a rash. What tube are you talking about?"

Malik pouts at the rebuke. "Well, I got a tube once."

"You've never had surgery in your life."

"I read a lot. Those tubes can give you rashes."

Douglas is beginning to feel left out. "I think I got a rash. I need some of that cream Malik gets."

"You don't have a rash. That's just some redness from lying in bed a long time."

"I need that cream. You give it to Malik. How come I can't get it? This is discrimination! I know my rights!"

"So I take it your bowels are OK?"

Back to Malik. "Hey! I got constipation. Fierce. Excruciating."

Douglas senses an opportunity. "Can I get some more of those pink pills?"

I felt like piling all their medications in the middle of the room and letting them take their pick.

Sometimes the inmates abandon subtlety. Amber Pagano, one of the occasional female patients passing through the infirmary, hit me with this exchange as I entered her room.

"Morning, Ms. Pagano, how are things going today?"

"Just give me my fucking Percocets."

"Tell me about—"

"I don't need any of this shit! Just give me my drugs!"

Guess we'd narrowed down the priorities here.

SEVENTEEN

BREAKING INTO PRISON

W ho would want to work in a prison? Well, me for one, but I'm a special case. Back when they were called guards, turnkeys, or screws at Colorado Territorial Prison, the "Old Max" of the 1800s, COs came mostly from retired men who either needed a job or were driven to more congenial surroundings by their home lives. There was no age requirement, and guards were frequently in their seventies, drawing a salary of $25 a month.

Today's correctional officers, no longer called guards, come from a more diverse pool. A minority want to go into law enforcement as a career, and some have degrees in criminal justice. FBI or other law enforcement aspirants may need a couple of years of field experience before proceeding with their careers.

Some come from a military background and like the structure and discipline of the job. Others, retired from an earlier career, are looking for a double-dip retirement fund. A large number have this as their first real job and came here from a history of flipping burgers or delivering pizzas. Many have had irregular or seasonal jobs like construction and are looking for a steady paycheck.

We get retirees looking to supplement their savings in a bleak economy. Most need the benefit package of health insurance and retirement plan as much as they need the paycheck. In other words, they come from everywhere with all different levels of experience for every reason under the sun.

The requirements? You have to be twenty-one, have a high school diploma, a Colorado driver's license, and no felony convictions. There are also some fairly minimal physical requirements that even I could pass. The pay? About $39,000 plus state benefits.

In the fine print are things like "Work in situations involving assaultive behavior, physical control of another person, and/or restraint situations." Hmmm? And "Deal with individuals with a range of moods and behaviors, utilizing tactfulness and a congenial personable manner." Right... Oh, and "Swing a baton in a striking technique." In a congenial personable manner, of course.

Prison guards were almost exclusively white males until the 1970s. Women served as matrons in the women's prisons or as clerical staff in men's facilities. Concern about the increasing population of minority and female inmates along with the civil rights movement broke the barrier to female and minority participation as correctional officers.

There was initial concern that female officers would not be physically up to the job and would not give adequate backup to their male counterparts. This certainly isn't the case at CSP, where female officers routinely handle the most dangerous offenders and are often more effective than their male counterparts at defusing dangerous situations without violence.

I don't know quite why this is. A CO always escorts the nurses when they take medications around on medline. They tell me they are much more likely to have trouble with inmates when accompanied by a big, strong male CO than if a petite female CO is along. The inmates seem more respectful and agreeable.

I asked if this was due to a sexual innuendo kind of thing, but they all said it was more of an "I'm not in competition with you" attitude. The same authority and control is there, but more like a mother and less like a father.

Female nurses frequently neutralize tense situations in a housing pod with verbal skills rather than brawn. They are able to joke with the inmate or simply say, "What do you think you're doing? You quit that right now." And the inmate quits. I think it's the "Mom Effect." When Mom talks, you listen. When Dad talks, sometimes you don't.

Minority representation in the ranks of correctional officers helps calm the waters as well. Black or Hispanic inmates no longer look out on a sea of white jailers, so some of the racial tension eases. The Hispanic officers and inmates in particular are a help to me in the form of instant translators. I do pretty well speaking Spanish, but if I get a rapid-fire street-lingo Latino jabbering at me, I get lost in a hurry.

Racism exists at CSP, but I've only seen it exhibited by the inmates. There's real vitriol about racial and religious differences, but it gets cut off at the knees pretty quickly if any of it shows up around the COs, particularly since their ranks are multi-racial too.

It's difficult to recruit high-quality people to work in corrections. The job has the "knuckle dragger" onus that's tough to ignore. The very real dangers of working in a prison setting make the occupation of corrections officer more toward the bottom of the list of things kids want to do when they grow up.

It's not too surprising when you have a new officer with a high school education up against the savviest cons in the world that many of the "fish" end up getting caught in compromising situations. It's not their fault in most cases, just lack of worldly experience. Overall I give the officers I work with high marks for professionalism. However, a few washed out of training because they wanted to be officers so they could "earn the big bucks" by being drug mules for the inmates.

COs are human. You have to harden yourself to work in a prison, especially in the supermax with feces flying, psychotic outbursts, and unprovoked violence. It can be tough to let the shield down at the end of the shift.

It's tough to keep the toxicity of the prison environment from bleeding into your private life. Correctional officers' life expectancy is around fifty-nine years, compared with seventy-seven for the overall U.S. population. The suicide rate is almost 40 percent higher than for other occupations.

Some let the abuse roll off, not take it personally, and leave the stress of the job at the gate. Others bottle it up inside, doing a slow burn that eats away at relations with family and friends. Depression and alcoholism are common. Domestic violence seems almost inevitable with abuse piled on every day, and yet the officers are forbidden to react in kind. Many complain of being short-tempered with their spouses and children. One told me, "I take a shower when I get home, but it won't come off."

Medline or "drugs for thugs" as the nurses call it, consists of dispensing medications to inmates twice daily. In a general population prison, the inmates line up at the clinic and get the medication through a window manned by a nurse on the inside and a CO on the outside. They watch to see that the medications aren't cheeked or pocketed instead of being taken on the spot.

At CSP it's room service. The nurses load up a cart with each inmate's medication and make the rounds of the pods accompanied by a CO. The CO is not there just to open the tray slot. He's the protection if an inmate makes a grab for the nurse's hand or has a surprise like a feces bomb when the slot is opened.

Feces (or urine) bombs are containers of the appropriate bodily substance which are either thrown from an open container or squeezed from a plastic bottle at the unwary victim through an open tray slot. It's one reason the inmates can't get large plastic bottles anymore.

Obviously this is hilarity of the first order, scoring lots of points for the perpetrator. Even though it busts the inmate back to Level One and brings criminal assault charges, for the lifers and the insane it doesn't make much difference.

Medline is also an occasion for further gaming the system. At CSP the inmates like to sleep in every morning. This makes it inconvenient for them to roll out and make it all the way to the tray slot to get their medication. Ergo, requests for medication to be dispensed at the afternoon medline. Randy Huber, a car thief with a violent streak, likes to party all night. Not being a morning person, he kited for an appointment.

"Doc, you gotta switch my meds to afternoon."

"Because...?"

"When I take those pills in the morning, I get sick. Bad stomach cramps. Sometimes I get a rash too. Itches like crazy. It's cool when I get them in the afternoon. So we can switch 'em?"

"No."

"No?"

"No."

"But I get cramps. Bad. Excruciating."

"Please."

Desperate, Randy pulls out all the stops. "This is cruel and unusual punishment. Deliberate indifference. This violates my rights. You gotta do this."

"Which rights would that be?"

Randy didn't expect a pop quiz. "You know. Rights. Civil rights. Human rights. I got rights!"

"You're a prisoner. You got morning medline. Deal with it."

B esides the COs, the nurses are the people in closest contact with the inmates. They're the eyes and ears of medical, and that's good. But sometimes things get a little too close for comfort. One of my nurse buddies, Vikki Muir, told me about this exchange with inmate Ryan, a gang kingpin in Denver.

"Nurse Muir, you're the only one's really cared about me. I just want you to know I appreciate it."

"Thank you, Mr. Ryan. We all try to do a good job."

"Yeah, but you're really special. Listen, if anyone's giving you trouble you just let me know."

"Trouble?"

"You know. Husband. Some asshole at the corner market. Anybody gives you trouble, you let me know. They be gone."

"Uh, thanks. I don't think I need anyone whacked right now."

"Anytime."

We're told on day one in training academy that the inmates will look for weaknesses and personal information they can exploit to get their hooks into you. A missing wedding ring, bags under the eyes, separation from coworkers. They're all potential signs of personal troubles that provoke a sympathetic response from the sharks.

Several times a year staff members will get "walked-out" for involvement with inmates. It always seems to start with a little sympathy from an inmate, which escalates into a friendship. This progresses to doing little favors, and it's all downhill from there.

It becomes either a romantic or power entanglement. A CO may become a drug mule either to get extra money or because of being in too deep. It's amazing how even experienced COs and nurses can get fatally attached to the dregs of society.

We lost one nurse last year to a prisoner who was in for life without parole for murder. He had seduced and compromised two nurses previously. We all knew it. She knew it. And yet she fell in love with this guy who was never going to see the light of day.

He used her as a runner for several months until the other staff noticed that she was spending a lot of extra time at his cell. The intel people started watching and pretty soon she was escorted to the parking lot by a couple of grim-faced former colleagues.

As a weird epilogue, she continued the relationship by mail and phone on the outside, even though the inmate was bragging about how he'd nailed another one. It was just a game to him. And he's got plenty of time to play it.

Most approaches are subtle, but some are a little more overt. Here's a prelude to my last clinic visit with Rollo Ortiz, a rapist from Durango.

"Nice watch, Doc."

"Thanks, Mr. Ortiz. Costco. Thirty bucks."

"I could get you a nice Rolex. Titanium. Diamonds. The whole bit."

"Good price, eh?"

"Just for you, Doc."

"Delivered?"

"Friend of mine'll get it for you."

"Gee, I don't know if I could trust anybody else as much as I trust you."

Ortiz senses that the bribe isn't working. "My back's killing me, Doc. Excruciating."

EIGHTEEN

MASTER CRIMINALS

Forty-five people enter Colorado prisons each day. One in three women and one in five men are incarcerated for a drug offense. So who are these inmates at the supermax? Lex Luthor? Hannibal Lecter? Probably the cream of the criminal crop, or so I thought.

In fact, these are the guys who managed to flunk out of regular prison. Most are violent offenders or sexual predators whose victims were inmates in other prison facilities. Some are gang members who have been put in the supermax to throw a crimp into their criminal organization. A few are placed here for their own protection; inmates who are habitually victimized by others or inmates who have been marked for retribution by gangs for traitorous activity.

Some are transferred to the Colorado supermax from other states because there is no safe place to keep them on their home turf. Whenever I call up a computer record on one of these inmates, a big red box pops up warning me to tell nobody about who or where they are. See Appendix A for a list...just kidding.

Original offenses range from kidnapping, child molesting and murder down to relatively minor crimes involving drugs or car theft. We even have white collar types. Check forgers, embezzlers, equity skimming, and exhibitionists are here. Even habitual traffic offenders.

The common denominator is an inability to get along in a general prison population. These are the guys you see on TV shows viciously attacking prison staff or other inmates, often with little or no reason. They are people of diverse backgrounds but with the common trait of a total lack of empathy. The concept of consideration for another human being is totally unknown in the supermax population. It's a continual sociopath convention.

One of my recent admissions to CSP, a supposedly trusted inmate at the Limon prison, ambushed and murdered a young CO. The reason? He wanted to increase his status in the prison by killing a cop.

As I waded into the world of dealing medically with these people, I would find myself talking with a man who had committed horrendous crimes only to realize he hadn't a smidgen of guilt or compassion for those he had injured. I seldom heard protestations of innocence, but often heard complaints about the injustice of their incarceration for their crimes. They really didn't see anything wrong with what they had done.

If the inmate stabbed someone to death, it was the victim's fault for not giving up his wallet, thereby forcing the perpetrator to kill him. If someone objected to having his car stolen, it was only right that he be shot. If a woman resisted his sexual advances, of course he would have to teach her a lesson. What else was he supposed to do?

A hallmark of the sociopathic personality is to have this lack of connection with other people. Sociopaths believe they are entitled to whatever they want at that particular moment, and they are completely justified in using any means to obtain it. If somebody gets in their way, well, that's the victim's fault.

When I saw these men as patients, I was frequently struck by their agreeable and engaging nature. Until I said "no" to what they wanted. Then their Jekyll and Hyde personalities would flip and I'd be sitting in front of true evil revealed.

As a rule, supermax inmates are consummate con men. Many are bright, and a frightening percentage are extremely charismatic.

When I first came to CSP I treated Ajax, a large, imposing man with wild whips of hair and a booming voice who was being treated with several medications for seizures. It didn't take long to realize he didn't have seizures at all. He was simply gaming the system for drugs.

I cut off his medications and all hell broke loose. Suddenly Ajax was having "seizures" day and night, inflicting bruises and small mutilations on himself, filing grievances and generally being a huge pain about his "severe epilepsy."

I wondered about his insistence that he had seizures when it was obvious that he didn't. I broke my vow of ignorance and looked back in his arrest record. The fog lifted.

It seems Ajax picked up a new acquaintance, Jones, at a bar one night and invited him to go camping. Don't ask me why Jones would think an invitation to go camp in the middle of the night with a stranger was a good idea, but he did. Later, Jones was found stabbed to death.

At trial, Ajax insisted he had been attacked by his new acquaintance. He had started to defend himself but had a sudden seizure, causing him to accidentally stab his new buddy thirty-seven times.

Suddenly, Ajax's insistence on having a seizure disorder made more sense. Sort of. The jury didn't buy it, and I didn't either.

When he came to the clinic he would throw himself on the floor, writhing and jerking with one eye on his audience. This went on until I asked him to be careful not to trip anyone in the clinic while he was having one of his spells.

His next stunt was to strip naked and climb halfway up a ten-foot chain link fence in the yard. It was a little difficult to know how to handle this. Nobody wanted to go up after him, so we let him hang there. After almost an hour he got tired and climbed down to a waiting pair of handcuffs. I'm not sure what this had to do with his seizures, but at least it was a break in the routine.

When his sentence was up he declared he was off to Texas to be a preacher. And apparently he was. A dozen acolytes, complete with banners, guitars, and tambourines, met him at the bus stop. They all loaded into a van and headed for the border, kumbayaing all the way. He's probably got his own television show now.

———

It's tough to control a man who's got nothing to lose. Therefore, one of the key features of the CSP program is giving an offender something to lose.

You have to remember that the inmates of CSP have earned their way there. These are the guys who have been yanked out of regular, general population prisons because of bad behavior.

With this prison demotion comes a loss of most of the ordinary privileges people take for granted. The program at CSP, however, lets you earn them back.

When a new offender arrives at CSP, he starts at Level One. He can work his way up to Level Three at CSP if he behaves. That means increased access to canteen items, more visitation opportunities, library books, and other little niceties that become super important when you've got lots of free time. If good behavior continues he can advance to Levels Four through Six via a transfer to the less restrictive Close Custody of Centennial next door. It usually takes an inmate a minimum of two years to work his way out of CSP.

At Level One the inmate lives in a solitary cell without books, TV, mail, or any personal items except for basic hygiene. If he behaves for a full seven days he can advance to Level Two. At this point, he gets a thirteen-inch black and white TV set in a supposedly shatter-proof Lexan case, which gets the local channels and the programs for rehabilitation that the prison provides. Now he's got something to lose.

The emphasis at CSP is on cause-and-effect. If an offender screws up, the consequences are immediate. If a prisoner cusses me out for some reason, I can pull his TV set for three days. Right then. No trial. No paperwork.

Now that might not sound like a big deal, but with nothing else to do 24/7, it's a huge deal. Especially during football season. It's amazing how much behavior improves during the playoffs. Huge.

The fact that the effect comes hard on the heels of the cause is a great reinforcement. Action. Consequence. A large number of these guys have no concept of delayed gratification. They want it. They take it. No thought process in between the two.

When dealing with the attention span of a fruit fly, an immediate virtual slap upside the head works wonders. Inmates begin to realize that their own actions, not something that someone else did to them, resulted in the consequence. It's a concept most kids pick up and internalize in kindergarten, but it's entirely foreign to the CSP crowd.

Tim Tebow, the former Denver quarterback, was scheduled for his debut performance in a Sunday game against the Detroit Lions in early September. The Friday before the game, I told offender Martin Grable that he wasn't getting a cane for his sprained ankle. He didn't take the news graciously.

As Martin hobbled back to his cell from the pod medical exam room, feet shackled and handcuffs secured behind his back, he decided that assaulting the two officers escorting him would be the appropriate response. He head-butted the one on his right and attempted to kick the one on the left, tripping himself in the process.

Officers at CSP have a low tolerance for such things. Before I could even think of sounding an alarm, three other COs erupted from the pod office. Martin was crushed under a half ton of angry blue uniforms before he could scream police brutality. I didn't see a lot of PPCT kinder-and-gentler control techniques being applied, but maybe I was just too far away to appreciate their subtlety.

The upshot of this episode was an immediate demotion of Martin's Level Three status down to a Level One. No discussion. No presentation to a disciplinary panel in three weeks. Now! This included confiscation of his TV set. Martin was a Broncos fan, and the loss of his TV was almost more than he could bear.

Sunday came. He howled. He cried. He cursed. He kicked his cell door with his sprained ankle. Tebow didn't play and the Broncos lost 25-20 in the last ninety seconds. Martin was convinced they would have won with his support, but he was also dimly aware that head-butting the CO wasn't his best move.

Cause and effect, not, "This is somebody else's fault." It entailed linking actions with consequences in the most immediate fashion. Out of small realizations like this come more substantial behavior changes. At least that's what CSP shoots for. Sometimes it even works.

C SP inmates are famous for being tightly contained and then deto-
nating in violence. Sometimes I can see it coming. If blood pressure, pulse, and respirations are way up, I know the inmate is having
a bad day even before I walk into the room. That may mean he has a
similar experience in mind for me.

My old buddy, Martin Grable, the Broncos fan whose TV I confiscated, was scheduled to see me for a checkup on his cholesterol. When
the nurse brought in his vital sign sheet, everything was off the charts,
like he'd just run a mile before hitting the exam room. Remembering
the head-butting incident that got his TV confiscated, I was wary.
Surely he didn't blame me for that. Probably no hard feelings about not
getting a cane either. Sure.

When I came into the exam room Martin had his head down, glar-
ing at me under knitted eyebrows, mouth set in a grim line. That in
itself didn't set Martin apart from lots of other inmates with attitude,
but the numbers were a tip-off. I'm usually right up next to my patients
when I do my exams, listening to the heart, leaning over the shoulder
to catch breath sounds. Not today.

Sure enough, I felt his muscles tense as he lunged toward me from
his seat on the gurney. I sidestepped and Martin pitched ass over ap-
plecart onto the floor. The two COs were on him like Dobermans on a
steak. I hopped back as he tried to bite me in the leg. Grudges last a long
time in the big house. Martin got his TV confiscated again.

Attacks like this one are rare, but minor skirmishes are common.
I've had inmates slap my hand away during an exam. CDOC considers
this an assault on an officer, but I rarely take this to the next level of
writing them up or bringing other charges unless there's real attitude
behind the slap. The inmates don't mean to injure me; they just want to
be left alone.

Threats are another matter. I get threatened all the time. They usually stop short of an explicit promise to beat me up or kill me, but I
routinely field comments about what would happen if I wasn't seeing

the inmate within the safety of a prison surrounded by guards. Most of these are muttered invectives as they're being escorted from an unsuccessful drug-seeking visit.

If I'm feeling a little testy, I'll ask them to speak up and repeat what they just said. They seldom do, but sometimes it leads to a real outburst of vitriol against the prison, COs, the food, thin mattresses, and, most especially, the crap medical care they're getting. This is usually enough to get them a time-out period over in Intake and a write-up with at least temporary loss of privileges.

Not long ago I saw Julius Glass, a temperamental survivalist who shot a game warden who he felt was infringing upon his constitutional rights. He started right in. No small talk.

"I need a thicker mattress. I got chronic back pain. It's in the chart."

"I understand you have back pain. You get one mattress like everyone else."

"At Limon (another Colorado prison) they gave me two mattresses. They said I'd get the same thing here."

Even though I knew the result, I flipped through the chart. "Nope. Nothing here from Limon about double mattresses."

"Bullshit. I had two there. You're a lying sack of shit, just like that other bitch."

"Excuse me?"

"You heard me. You're so fucking cheap, you get these crap mattresses I wouldn't get for my dog. Why don't *you* try one?"

"I think we're done here," I said, motioning to the COs.

"We ain't done here," he yelled. "I want that fucking mattress. If I don't get it you'll be getting a visit." Now he'd crossed the line.

"Really? A visit from who?"

"I got friends."

"That's great. Maybe they can be character witnesses at your trial."

"What fucking trial?"

"You just threatened a peace officer. That's a felony."

"Just try it, smartass."

"Done. Maybe they can tell you how the Broncos game came out too."

I don't usually take these episodes too seriously. Maybe one day a former patient will meet me in a dark alley with revenge in his heart, but it doesn't seem likely. Most will have more pressing problems to deal with, like finding shelter or something to eat. Still, if one day I turn up with multiple gunshot wounds, there'll be a long list of suspects.

NINETEEN

CONTRABAND

You might think with everyone locked in solitary confinement 23/7, illegally transferring material from one place to another might be a problem. Not really.

The mail is monitored, of course. All letters are opened and inspected before delivery. Pretty basic. But it's easy to saturate a predetermined area of a letter with LSD; invisible to the naked eye, but readily harvested and used or sold.

A dose of black tar heroin is about the size of the period at the end of this sentence and easily placed on the undersurface of a stamp.

One enterprising smuggler meticulously sliced a postcard in half sideways. He made a heroin sandwich from the two halves, which he mailed to his inmate buddy. It didn't make it through, but it was a damn good job.

Since legal mail is exempt from searches, a popular dodge is sending information to a lawyer who then forwards it on to the real recipient. Return mail is handled by the same route. Some inmates have gone to the trouble of forming their own law firm on the outside to handle their traffic.

The internal drug distribution system is a little different in the supermax compared to a general population prison. In general population, prisoners circulate among one another and pass contraband directly. Likewise, friends and relatives frequently pass contraband during visits. Cameras and COs often catch these passes, but some always slips through.

Sad to say, the COs are sometimes the source. The offenders are absolute master con men. They watch and listen constantly and know an astounding amount of personal information about those guarding them.

What time you come and go to work: "You're working pretty hard. I saw you leave late last night."

Where you live: "How's the weather in Pueblo?"

What children you have: "Cute drawing you put up in the office, Lieutenant. I've got a kid about that age. Boy or girl?"

What kind of car you drive: "Saw the new SUV you drove in today. Nice wheels. I used to have one just like that. "

The sudden absence of a wedding ring: "I've had some problems at home too."

A change of clothing or hair style: "Hey, you're really looking sharp today. Lose some weight?"

A change in attitude: "A little blue today, Sarge? I know how tough it can be. The economy and all."

A problem with co-workers: "Those guys are all assholes, aren't they?"

Got a Broncos sticker on your car? "Say, did you see the game last weekend?"

The purpose of all this is not casual or friendly. They're always setting you up for something. And they've got time to do it. Months and months, even years and years. Nothing but time.

Setting you up for what? Anything. Want an extra pillow? A special snack? How about that extra magazine? Do you think you could get me that green pill for another couple of weeks? How about a quick hand job through the tray slot? Could you just mail this letter for me?

So how does it happen that people who are basically law-abiding and have passed a fairly rigorous background check end up catering to a lifer in a maximum-security cell? Easy. Here's a scenario. It really happened.

An offender had singled out a newly hired officer as someone he could exploit. The officer was chewing gum as he made his rounds. Gum is contraband in the supermax, but the new hire either didn't know or just slipped up.

The officer passed the offender's cell. "Where's mine?" the con said.

"Where's your what?"

"The gum, man. Where's my piece?"

"What are you talking about? I got no gum for you."

"Not supposed to have gum in here, man. You know that."

Now the new CO is in a tough place. Either he didn't know and thinks maybe he should have, or he does know and realizes he slipped up.

The offender smiles. "Hey, man. I don't want to get you in trouble by reporting this. Just give me a piece and we'll call it even."

The intelligent thing to do is for the CO to blow off the offender and then tell the pod sergeant about his mistake in bringing a piece of gum in. Things happen. Honest mistake. Not a big deal. But, nooooooo...

You can write the rest of this story. The offender gets the piece of gum, but more importantly he's got his hooks into the CO. Every time it gets to be a little more.

Pretty soon it's a snack or a magazine. "Mail this letter for me, will you? I don't have a stamp." This, of course, is to bypass the mail censors.

End of story is the CO gets in deeper and deeper. He ends up running heroin in his lunchbox. Eventually somebody suspects, then surveillance confirms. The CO gets busted and ends up as a guest of the same prison system as all the nice folks he was guarding.

The punishment for the offender? "Hey, man, I ain't never gettin' out of here. What you gonna do to me?" He's right.

One lady, employed as a teacher at the Sterling prison, was caught with her bra stuffed full of cigarettes. Alcohol smuggling is more of a challenge, but isn't all that hard to do, even by accident.

COs usually bring lunches or dinners to work and stow them in the pod refrigerator. One day, at the end of a shift, a lone can of beer stood on the top shelf. A mistaken grab from the home refrigerator no doubt, but nobody was going to claim it.

One time I was startled in the middle of clinic by a telephone ringing in my tote bag. Sure enough, I had smuggled a cell phone into the supermax prison without even knowing it, passing the front lobby staff, x-ray, and metal detectors along the way.

———

Inmates love drugs. Many of the requests I got came from watching ads on TV. By now there isn't a male in the Western Hemisphere who hasn't been made aware of his strangling prostate gland. As it happens, there are wonderful drugs that relieve all the symptoms you didn't know you had until you saw the commercials. A case in point was Wyatt Desoto, a gangbanger from Florida.

"Hey, Doc, I need to get me some of that (he quickly looks at a scrap of paper balled in his hand) Ditropan. Yeah, I got all the stuff they talk about."

"And that would be....?"

"You know. All that stuff."

"Could you help me out on that one? I don't have a checkbox on my form for 'all that stuff.'"

And so it goes. TV commercials popularize the Next Great Thing in medical science. It grows hair. It gives you baby-smooth skin. It cures warts and cancer. Suddenly my entire convict population has "all that stuff." And they want it treated. Right now. Thank you.

Of course 99 percent have nothing that the Next Great Thing is designed to treat and wouldn't know it if they did have it. But certain diseases and their attendant medications fall in and out of fashion with the prison population. It primarily rests on somebody's report that "If you grind up the blue pill and snort it, man, it will blow your mind. And if you can mix it with one of the red ones, you're on a rocket!"

It doesn't seem to matter what the actual pharmacology of the medication is. It's all in the hype. We've got downers that inmates use as uppers and vice versa.

It's called the placebo effect. If I give someone an aspirin and tell them it's a powerful sedative, it will be. He'll be fighting to keep his eyes open. Give the same aspirin with a caution that it's really going to rev them up, and they won't sleep for a week. Mind (sort of) over matter.

Since business in pharmaceuticals thrives within these walls, I had to look at a sudden outbreak of urinary retention in twenty-year-olds with some skepticism. Usually this disorder doesn't happen until men hit their golden years.

It was probably just a coincidence that there were tons of TV ads aired at that time about this very problem. Could it be that these men weren't being truthful? But then again, some people actually *did* have the disorder. The answer: crush and float.

When a medication is on our "abused" list, but I think somebody might really need it, I order the medication as C&F, that is "crush and float." This means the nurses crush up the pill and dissolve it in water. The inmate chugs this instead of swallowing the pill.

Most medicines taste terrible. It's a medical tradition. With C&F this effect is magnified. It also frustrates the snorters, pill hoarders, and entrepreneurs. It's tough to cheek a pill or secrete it in your clothes if it's liquid. Because of this, those who really don't need the medication drop it fairly quickly. "Hey, Doc, I'm all better!!"

Some entrepreneurial spirits find a way around this problem. If the staff is inattentive the inmate dumps the C&F liquid in a cup and evaporates it to recover the medication to snort or shoot up.

Even more inventive are the knowledgeable ones who read their home health guidebooks and know that certain medications are excreted unchanged in the urine. Take the med, pee into a cup, evaporate the liquid and get a two-for-one. Or three or four depending on your dedication to recycling. Usually it's one for you and one to sell.

Sir William Osler is often called the Father of Modern Medicine for his contributions to medical education. He stated, "The desire to take medicine is perhaps the greatest feature which distinguishes man from animals." I wonder if he ever worked in a prison.

But is this a surprise? It is not. The vast majority of my patients came into the prison system with extensive drug experience. And, face it, prison can be boring.

Although the medications we dispense are a great source of entertainment, the old reliables—methamphetamine, cocaine, and heroin—are still at the top of the list. The main sources of drugs in prison are contact visits and, unfortunately, staff.

Contact visits, as you might guess, are visits where the inmate and visitor can actually touch each other. At CSP we didn't have contact visits. The inmates visited on either side of a big sheet of Lexan while talking on a wall phone in a three-sided booth. Not a lot of opportunity to pass contraband. As a result, CSP has only a tenth of the drug problem that a general population prison like Fremont has.

However, even though there's no contact at CSP, visitors are searched prior to entry. Remember that inmates and their accomplices are endlessly inventive. The appearance of a gun or shiv, a homemade knife, in the visiting room is not unknown, and smuggling contraband of every description goes on constantly.

A visitor might hand the contraband to a complicit guard, go through the search and then the guard hands it back to her on the other side. And what happens if little Johnny has the hash in his diaper?

Easy to smuggle, easy to hide, and potent as hell, black tar heroin is always a favorite. A single hit of it is so tiny that it can be hidden almost anywhere. Like most prison drugs, direct injection into a vein is the most popular medium. Needles, homemade and otherwise, get passed around by ratlines. As a consequence, hepatitis C is as popular as heroin.

Between the intravenous drug use and tattoos, hepatitis C is endemic at the supermax. A chronic disease, there is no immunization for it and the treatment is imperfect, prolonged, debilitating, and expensive. Nevertheless, there's a steady stream of applicants who have experienced a medical epiphany and decided they need treatment. Right now.

"Ya gotta treat me, Doc! It's gonna kill me. I can feel it eatin' up my insides. I'm gettin' faint. Dizzy spells. Headaches. Warts. All that stuff."

Of course, the speaker has had Hep C for years and has no intention of giving up the drugs and tattoos that will give it right back to him again even if treated.

Such is the drama and amazement of the newly diagnosed. "It can't be, Doc. I always wore a rubber."

"You don't get it from sex. You get it from the drugs (pointing to the armful of blown veins) and the tattoos (trying to find a patch of unmolested skin anywhere)."

True to the ethos that it's always someone else's fault, the conversation quickly degenerates into, "Who gave it to me?" You did, Ace.

———————

I nmates are endlessly inventive in constructing weaponry. From your basic knife or shiv to bombs and guns, creativity flourishes.

In 1942 two Territorial inmates were blown to bits by a bomb consisting of a baby food jar filled with black powder. Inmates smuggled the powder little by little from the quarry operation behind the prison. The assassins ignited the powder by a fuse of cardboard matches woven together. A blank .22 caliber cartridge triggered by a rubber band secured underneath the jar on a steel spring provided the firing mechanism. The assassin handed the "gift" to the victims, triggered the device and ran like hell. Before they could react, the victims were toast.

In another prison, a sudden surge in religious interest aroused suspicions among the guards. They found the lower arm of the crucifixes made in the prison workshop actually formed a sheath for a wicked ice pick blade inside.

In the tradition of the Wild West, bows and arrows are common. One enterprising inmate made a functional crossbow firing steel shafts over fifty feet. The bow can be powered by elastic from underwear with arrows constructed from anything stiff and pointed. Moistened paper, rolled and dried, makes a great shaft.

Inmates make zip guns from radio aerials using rubber bands and nails to ignite a homemade cap with ammunition of steel fragments propelled by match heads. A sharpened toothbrush or part of a plastic food tray becomes a deadly shiv. One vengeful inmate made a blowgun out of paper with HIV-infected darts. Even a plastic bag can be lethal, the inmate heating the bag while slowly rolling it into a tapering spike. When it hardens, he's got a wicked weapon that doesn't trip metal detectors. The list is limited only by time and imagination, and the inmates have plenty of both.

Staff members bring in weapons, either accidentally or on purpose. Materials that might get thrown in the trash can end up in an inmate's arsenal. Compromised staff might bring in weapons for their inmate handlers. It's not that hard.

I'm a packrat with my tote bag. Books, PDA, lunch, CDs, sheaves of papers; its Fibber McGee's closet with a strap. Unless I happen to run into SORT team day with strip searches and sniffer dogs, I could probably bring a .357 in my bag and not get picked up.

Even though everyone is searched and goes through metal detectors every time they pass through the portals of the prison, after a while it becomes routine. It would be easy enough for staff to bring in weapons or contraband. Everybody knows everybody else, and who's going to suspect old Joe of bringing a stash of cocaine in his lunch bag? Unfortunately, sometimes that's exactly what old Joe does. Welcome to reality.

———◆———

Alcohol has been a part of human existence forever, and jail is no exception. Even though it's contraband, alcohol will continue to be in prison life because (1) inmates want it and (2) it's really easy to make. All you need is something that will ferment, and a little time.

Homebrew in prison goes by lots of different names like hooch, jump, jack, chalk, buck, and pruno. Pruno comes from the original recipe using prunes, but now the name applies to any fruit-based brew. Wardens at some prisons tried to curtail this by banning fruit from the meals, but they soon found the inmates making pruno from cake frosting, bread, jelly, and milk.

A classic pruno recipe consists of oranges, fruit cocktail, sugar, and ketchup. It's brewed in a plastic bag over a period of a week to ten days and kept warm by wrapping it in towels after heating it in hot water. Although I've never had the pleasure, I'm told it tastes like week-old vomit with a kick.

A more modern variant uses orange juice concentrate and adds dinner rolls to the mix for the yeast content. It does speed up the fermenting process but does absolutely nothing to improve the taste.

One of the more surprising ingredients used at CSP is orange-flavored Metamucil. It turns out that the flavored Metamucil has a fair amount of sugar in it. Our chief medical officer brewed up a batch to see if it really worked. It did, but it still looked and smelled like a swamp. Prisoners are desperate men.

TWENTY

GANGS AND TATTOOS

Tattoos or "tats" are big business in the big house. It's rare to find an inmate without a riot of dark blue figures and symbols covering his body. Nothing is exempt. You haven't really seen art until you've witnessed a phoenix on a penis.

Most are surprisingly good. Elaborate designs with obvious craftsmanship are the rule, but there are the amateur jobs as well. Skulls, guns, and knives are popular themes. Prophetically, chains and bars are well represented too. Women in various stages of undress gaze imploringly from forearms. An amazing number of inmates have their own names tattooed prominently on their chests, as if they might need a quick reference.

Tattoos are important gang signs. It seems you're not really a gang unless you sport your own distinctive tattoo. Most originated on the streets and became part of the prison culture. Crips, Bloods, Folk Nation, People Nation—all the major city gangs and the hundreds of splinter groups are represented with appropriate tats.

Sometimes the gang reference is overt with a "SURENO" or "13" prominently displayed. The "MM" or the black hand symbols of the Mexican Mafia are easy to pick out. Hard-core members use flamboyant gang tattoos mostly for the intimidation factor. If a pretender to the gang shows up with the wrong tattoo, the offending symbol is removed free of charge by the gang members via cutting or burning it off.

Because intel can pick out gang members by their markings, gang tattoos may be more subtle with a symbol hidden as part of another design. A discreet Norteno XIV tucked into a gun barrel. An Aryan Brotherhood shamrock adorning a knife hilt. Some are camouflaged within the hairline, only revealed with a head shave.

A confusing gaggle of numbers exists in tats as well, often related to penal codes for different types of crimes; 187 is a homicide in California, 211 for armed robbery. Numbers also correspond to positions of letters in the alphabet; 274 translates to BGD for the Black Gangster Disciples. Not to be too obvious, a 67 adds up to 13, which is a symbol for the ultra-violent MS-13 gang. Other numbers may indicate area codes of home gangs; anything to claim turf.

A popular tat is a teardrop at the corner of the eye. I don't claim to know what it means at this point. Originally, an open teardrop indicated that the wearer had killed someone. A closed teardrop meant he had lost a friend or relative. More recently, a half-closed teardrop was supposed to mean that a friend or relative of the wearer had been killed and the wearer had killed the attacker.

Now everyone seems to have a teardrop and the meaning has been essentially lost through dilution and wannabeism.

Dots are another common tat. They have the advantage of being simple and less painful to apply. Usually in the web of the hand or on the wrist, three dots in a triangle supposedly mean the three places the gang member can go—prison, hospital, or grave. Sometimes a single dot on the other hand can mean Surenos. Not obvious? Also known as Sur 13. Still don't get it? One dot and three dots. One and three. Oh, yeah. Surprised I didn't pick up on that one right away.

Of course, other gangs and wannabes picked up on the dot motif too. Some Hispanic gangs use it to mean "mi vidaloca," "my crazy life." Asian gangs use it to mean "To O Can Gica" or "I care for nothing." Others use it to mean their specialty is burglary. Now, like the teardrop, nobody knows what the dots mean. Maybe we should confine it to care-less Asian burglars.

As on the street, gangs are a fact of prison life. Originally formed for protection against other gangs, they quickly morphed into purveyors of the big three—power, sex, and drugs. Organized along racial lines, the black, white, Hispanic, and Asian gangs run the show.

Whether it's the Mexican Mafia or the Aryan Brotherhood, the motives are the same. They're engaged in criminal activity.

Well, duh! After all, who's locked up in the prisons anyway? But now the criminal activity is directed toward the prison facility, its staff and programs.

Before 1982 when it became illegal, there existed a "building tender" system where trustees, usually older white men who had been inmates for long periods of time, would maintain order through spying and intimidation. Stepping into the void, gangs now maintain their own brand of order using the same tools.

Make no mistake. These are not nice people. These are not social clubs. For many of the gangs it's "blood-in, blood-out." This means that an initiate must kill someone to get into the gang, and the only way out is by his own death.

Rank in the organization is no protection. When Ernesto "Smokey" Miranda, one of the founders of MS-13, declined to attend a party for a member who had recently been released from prison, he was gunned down in his home. Miranda had been studying law and working to keep children out of gangs.

Most gangs have formal organization with a written constitution, bylaws, and elected officials. The Bloods and Crips, both African-American gangs, are exceptions with no written structure. Because of this they are classified as "security threat groups" instead of gangs.

There's really no difference as far as the danger these groups represent, but the prison administration makes a distinction because they can use the gang's structure or lack of it as a means of predicting and controlling behavior. For instance, if part of a gang's bylaws provide for ways to distribute income, prison intel people can trace the flow of money to shed light on gang leadership.

If they weren't so deadly, the sheer number of splinter gangs and their names would be funny. The white supremacist Aryan Brotherhood grew from the Blue Bird Gang. Small wonder they changed that.

Last time I counted, the Bloods had 118 splinter gangs, edging out the Crips at 115. They have to stretch to come up with some of their names, and they seem to keep morphing all the time. For instance, the Dub-Trey Gangsters were formerly known as the CCNHB, but also as the Rollin' 20s and the 317 Bloods. How do you keep track? You need a scorecard to know which gang you're in. And think of the embarrassment of having last year's name tattooed on your butt.

I have a special fondness for one group since it originated in Indianapolis, my hometown. They frequently wear Atlanta Braves hats, because they have an "A" on them. You know. "A" for Indianapolis. I love these guys.

Salvadorans fleeing the death squads in civil-war-plagued El Salvador formed the nucleus of one gang. When they migrated to California they formed MS-13 or Mara Salvatrucha as protection against rival Mexican gangs.

Nobody is quite sure what Mara Salvatrucha means. Some say the name comes from *La Mara*, a street in San Salvador. The word *mara* means gang in Caliche, a local Salvadorian dialect. This in turn is taken from *marabunta*, a kind of army ant. Another interpretation is that it derives from a combination of the words *Salvadoran* and *trucha*, a Caliche word for being alert. If you translate the words Mara Salvatrucha literally into English, it comes out something like "saving trout." That's probably not what they had in mind.

MS-13 members are famous for imbedding every square inch of their bodies, including their faces, with tattoos. When considering the real estate required for the full name, it's no wonder that many opt for the shorter MS-13 or just 13 or 67.

When it comes to violence and cruelty, MS-13 ranks at the top. They are so violent that other gangs hire them to do their dirty work. When the Honduran government proposed restoring the death penalty, MS-13 reacted by ambushing a bus, spraying it with automatic fire from six members, then boarding the riddled vehicle and systematically executing anyone who had survived the onslaught. Most of the twenty-eight passengers were women and children.

Violence in the pursuit of their various businesses is somewhat understandable, but the sheer viciousness of the MS-13 members goes way beyond that. In San Francisco, a car briefly blocked an MS-13 member, Miguel Ramos, from making a left-hand turn onto a narrow street. Ramos got out, shot and killed the forty-eight-year-old driver and his two teenage sons for the inconvenience.

They are proud of their reputation. One of their leaders wrote in an intra-gang communication: "Wherever the Mara Salvatrucha is, we are going to kill, control, and rape again. We are super crazy." Hard to argue with that.

MS-13 members often spend time in U.S. prisons and are then deported to El Salvador where they spend time in Ciudad Barrios prison, sort of a college for MS-13 recruiting and training. Then it's back to the U.S. illegally for another round of recruiting in the U.S. prisons. Not being as creative as some other gangs, factions of MS-13 frequently name themselves after Los Angeles streets like the Temple Street, Diamond Street, or Witmer Street Gangs.

The Mexican Mafia, one of the first prison gangs to develop in the United States, is a pro-Hispanic gang founded, like most of the gangs, in California. The Texas branch was founded by Herbie Huerta, a former spiritual leader of the Mexikanemi Science Temple of Aztlan, a mouthful in any language.

Herbie expressed his desire to establish a Hispanic network based on "character" with an emphasis on love over hate. Herbie was serving three life terms for murder, conspiracy, and racketeering at the time. A perfect fit.

The Mexican Mafia is heavy into drugs, with an emphasis on heroin. Their favorite tactic is to recruit corrections officers as mules, giving them a 40 percent cut of the profits. I couldn't find any stories of drug mules at CSP, but contraband smuggling by staff happens. As long as people are involved, no system is completely secure. How can Charles Manson get two cell phones in the heavily guarded Protective Housing Unit of California's Corcoran Prison?

Where there's money to be made, there's competition. La Nuestra Familia started in California's Folsom State Prison as an opposing group to the Mexican Mafia. They moved east and have developed strong ties within the Colorado prison system, particularly in Limon Penitentiary before the development of the CSP supermax.

More than most gangs, La Familia operates with a cause: protecting Chicano culture as well as its members from the predominately white population of the Colorado prisons.

La Familia seems like a kinder, gentler type of gang. With leaders named "Smiley" Garcia and "Happy" Cervantes, what could be more chummy? It's even organized as an all-American capitalist organization with a business manager, finance minister, security chief and everything. They run company stores for inmates to purchase items with a 150 percent payback rate for a week's credit and 200 percent after that. For reluctant debtors there are always the debt collectors.

Not so nice are the "Wolfpacks" recruited and trained in prison by Familia members. Once paroled, these members carry out the orders of their imprisoned bosses. Their responsibility is to generate revenue for the Familia by robbing banks, armored cars, or private homes.

You might think that gangs function like hate groups against other racial gangs. And you'd be right, unless it gets in the way of business.

That's why the Mexican Mafia (MM), La EME, is buddies with the Aryan Brotherhood (AB). Say what? You bet. It's because the Black Guerilla Family is in bed with Nuestra Familia.

La EME is, of course, a mortal enemy of La Nuestra Familia since both are composed of Mexican-Americans. It's only natural that they would turn to a white supremacist group for assistance. And it helps that the AB is very big into the sales of methamphetamine.

Now don't confuse the Mexican Mafia, La EME, with the *Texas* Mexican Mafia, the Mexikanemi or EMI. The Mexikanemi is also sometimes known as Mary Lou. Loosely translated, Mexikanemi means "Free Mexican." That's why they're in prison.

Now at the time of this writing the Mexikanemi have a peace agreement with the Mexican Mafia, but are mortal enemies of the *New*

Mexican Mafia and, of course, the Black Guerilla Family. You need a program to tell the players.

The supremacist groups like the Aryan Brotherhood, Aryan Syndicate, and 211 are the most prominent white gangs here at CSP. The Surenos, who are controlled by the Mexican Mafia, are the biggest players on the Hispanic side.

Where do all these gang members come from? A lot come from the streets. People often enter prison already affiliated with a gang. If an inmate is outnumbered or otherwise finds his gang affiliation is a disadvantage, he may switch gangs in prison and then switch back upon release.

There are also professional gang recruiters. Frequently they are top men in California gangs who travel to Colorado and commit a car theft or other relatively minor crime. They are then sentenced to a couple of years in the Colorado pokey.

While there, they quickly spread the word about who they are and how great it would be to become a member of (fill in the blank) gang. They pick local leaders and soldiers. When they get out they leave a nice profit center behind. Then it's off to New Mexico to steal a car and do the same thing all over again.

It's really hard to keep track of all the blood feuds going around. Fortunately, I don't have to. That's up to the guys and gals in Intelligence.

———

Between the sally ports to C-Pod is an office with blinds drawn behind small windows. An inconspicuous tag reads "Intel." Inside are the officers who not only catch the bad guys already in prison, they help catch their confederates on the street too. Sometimes they even catch other officers.

As inconvenient as it is to get busted for gang activity, smuggling, extortion and the like, it must be even worse to realize that you did it to yourself. Inmates just can't seem to keep their mouths shut.

For those of us who drive teenagers around, it's a familiar phenomenon. I'm in the front seat driving, while the gaggle of kids in the back spill their most intimate beans. If I don't comment on the conversation, I'm invisible; an automaton that just transports them from one place to another, hearing and seeing nothing.

I think it must be like that with the inmates. They don't see the intel guys, so they don't exist.

The prisoners know their mail is read, but still they put incriminating information in letters to their buddies on the outside. They might as well write out a confession and hand it to a CO. In fact, that's pretty much what they do.

An exception is mail to and from their attorneys. This is privileged information and bypasses the censors. Mostly. The officers "scan" the letter in front of the inmate, looking for contraband or obvious gang-related content, but unless something looks suspicious, they don't "read" it.

One dodge is for an inmate to send a privileged letter to his attorney. This attorney's job is to act as a mail drop. The attorney forwards the letter on to the actual recipient. The answering letter comes back by the reverse route. It doesn't take the intel folks long to pick up on who the attorney is and start reading the letters. It's especially obvious when a bunch of people in a gang are all using the same lawyer. Busted again.

Another ploy is the coded letter. The codes can get pretty sophisticated but often are simple substitution ciphers. Besides letters from the outside, inmates communicate internally with wellas. A wella is a note on a small piece of paper crammed with tiny writing. They're almost like engravings. I need a magnifying glass to read one.

Inmates pass the wellas by ratline or by wrapping them in plastic wrap and flushing them down the toilet. Now that might seem counterproductive, but there's a trick. The guy in the cell upstairs lets the guy below know that a message is on the way. The guy below flushes the end of a ratline down his toilet. The guy above flushes the wella. The two ratlines get all tangled up and the guy below reels it in. If he misses it, the guy upstairs gets to do another wella.

And then there's the telephone. Inmates can use a phone fixed to the wall of the housing pod. They're cuffed to a D-ring on the wall and can talk for ten minutes. This phone is part of the CIPS, the Colorado Inmate Phone System.

The calls are monitored. The intel listeners know who the inmates are, who they're calling, and can record the whole conversation. As a matter of fact, they do. They can monitor calls in any prison in the state.

When there's any kind of disturbance (prison-speak for riot) in a facility, the intel guys can go back and listen to all the phone calls to and from the prison to see just who was saying what to whom.

It must be something about the internet generation and their concept of anonymity. As soon as nobody is physically present on their shoulders, they think they're invisible, or in this case, inaudible.

The intel people have a field day. Drug deals, burglaries, where-I-hid-the-gun chat. It's astonishing the things they blab over an open line. Some seem to think that if they whisper, they won't get caught. Fish in a barrel.

Two-thirds of the inmates of CSP and Centennial are in gangs. Since they are major badasses, the leadership tends to be concentrated in the supermax prisons. The intel people have STG, Security Threat Group, files on all of them. File cabinets full. Row on row. Some have a single sheet of paper. Others have multiple folders stuffed with intelligence. Want to know who's related to whom, which gang is cozying up to another, what kind of contraband or extortion somebody's into? It's all in there.

The information for intel comes from multiple sources. Intercepted notes or mail and tapped phone calls comprise a constant flow of goodies. At the same time, the inmates themselves give away a ton of information through their relations with other inmates known to be gang members, or just from bragging.

Anybody who wants to visit an inmate at CSP has to fill out an application form and be approved. That means a background check by the intel people. I can hear what you're thinking. The answer is yes.

It's amazing how many wanted felons fill out an application to visit and submit it along with a driver's license. The cops either go to the address on the license and arrest them or just wait until they show up for their visit and invite them in to stay. Master criminals...

Respect tops the list of gang member needs. No respect equals no status. To get the respect, somebody else has to know that you deserve some. You can't hide under a rock and get respect. As the knowledge spreads regarding the movers and shakers, the so-called "shot-callers," inevitably the word gets to staff and intel.

Snitches play their roles as well, both inside the prison and out. Tips to the right people from a rival gang on the streets can fry the ambitions of someone inside the walls. Disgruntled relatives make phone calls to the warden. Information from other prisons regarding known associates or gang affiliations follows the convicts from one facility to another. People busted for offenses on the outside give up information about their prison buddies. On and on.

Intimidation and extortion are still problems even in a supermax situation like CSP. How can you intimidate another inmate when everyone is locked down 23/7 and there is never any physical contact? Easy. Here's an exchange reported to me by one of the COs.

Bad-Ass yells across the pod, "Hey, Smith. You got some stamps I can use?"

"I'm not givin' you any stamps."

"Your sister's name is Evelyn. She's twenty-three years old and lives at 123 South Street in Pueblo. Her phone number is 719-456-7891. Drives a five-year-old Honda. She's got a cute little white terrier named Maxie. What's Maxie weigh, Smith? Five pounds tops. Not much protection there."

"How many stamps you need?"

We have another famous inmate who likes boys. He's a mountain of a man and can get inmates in the cells across from his to strip and perform sex acts for him just by the intimidation factor of his gaze. That and his gang connections.

The threat is not that the victim is going to be harmed now. But just wait until he graduates into general population. Or he may be safe at CSP, but the gang members can get to his family on the outside.

TWENTY-ONE

"I AIN'T GONNA DO THAT!"

Hunger strikes are a common form of protest in prisons. They're usually over some perceived slight or disrespect, occasionally over the loss of privileges, rarely over anything that makes sense to anyone else.

As the presiding medico I'm required to meet with the starvees and explain to them the medical effects of not eating. The initial attitude is almost always a smug arrogance. "Look what I'm doing. I'm powerful. I've got the doctor in here. I'm going to get what I want."

I almost never get into the reason for their strikes. It just doesn't pay. They're looking for an audience, and I'm not that interested. I did ask one chubby guy who I'd seen recently why this sudden change in attitude. "I'm on a hunger strike because you won't give me extra snacks." That's why I don't ask.

In my conversation with them I try to stick to the way things are going to play. I tell them it's their choice how long to drag this thing out, but it's their choice only up to a point. As long as there's no medical emergency, they're free to abuse themselves as much as they want.

First a quick physical exam, including their weights. You'd be amazed how many inmates gain weight on a hunger strike. How? Preparation. They hoard snacks from the canteen before starting the strike or get them via ratlines from their buddies. They send back the meal trays and chow down on beef and cheese sticks. The strike ends when they run out of snacks.

I've never had a hunger striker go all the way and refuse water too. That would be too uncomfortable and wouldn't draw out the drama long enough. If that ever happens, I'll know they're really serious.

For the rest, I tell them that nothing much will happen for the first couple of weeks as long as they keep their fluids up. About week three or four, they'll start getting loopy. Then it's out of their hands and into ours. It's off to the hospital to get their fluids back in balance and force feed them with a tube. After they recover enough to be mentally competent, they're free to starve themselves into submission again.

Most strikers make it for a couple of weeks and then cave. A minority goes all the way to getting trucked to the hospital for force-feeding. Even this group usually chickens out when they see we're serious about stuffing a tube down their noses. Rarely do they pick up where they left off after returning to CSP.

They'll come up with a rationalization about how they've gotten what they wanted from whomever they wanted it from, but in reality all they've accomplished is to drop ten or fifteen pounds. Many then submit kites to be put on supplementary snacks because of unexplained weight loss. Really.

———

Compliance in the medical realm means how well the inmate is following the prescribed medication regimen. You might think that with almost free medical care, free medicines, and to-your-door delivery twice daily, following the program should be a snap. Apparently not.

There are lots of reasons inmates fall off the medical wagon. One of the most common is the I-don't-need-this-shit attitude. Many of our guests are young and therefore immortal. The idea that they have a disease that could kill or cripple them is such a foreign concept that they just reject it.

These are fairly easy to handle. They just don't get treated until the disease gets to the point that they wake up and smell the coffee. It's a basic tenet of medical care, in or out of prison, that a person has the right to refuse treatment as long as he's mentally competent to do so.

Like many of us, prisoners hate to get up in the morning. Often this means that when the nurses come around in the wee hours to distribute the morning medications, they won't get out of bed to take it.

Prison time schedules are skewed. If you go to a pod before noon, it's quiet as a termite at an aardvark convention. In the afternoon things get more rowdy as the night owls count out exercise cadences. Evening is TV and reading until well after midnight.

This means there are not a lot of early birds when morning medline comes around. Inmates are practiced at rolling out of bed, taking their pills, and slipping back under the covers in one fluid motion, but some just don't make the effort.

I talk to these guys about the importance of taking their medication; disease prevention, dire health consequences, yada, yada, yada. They insist they're taking them faithfully even though the labs and nurses' records show they're not. They blame the nurses for not bringing the medicine to them. They say the nurses bring the wrong medicines and they won't take them. They blame the high level of cosmic rays in the morning. They blame anything but their own behavior. So I end up taking them off the medications that they're not taking anyway.

Sometimes they don't care that they don't get their meds. Sometimes they raise all kinds of hell about how I'm denying them their rights. Bitching at the nurses. Nasty kites. Grievances. Threats of lawsuits. Anything but getting their sorry asses out of bed to take the free medicine. I don't lose a lot of sleep over these guys.

Then there's the group convinced we're trying to poison them. This is a brother organization to the toxic-fumes-through-the-vents crowd.

"It's a pink pill. I always get a blue pill." (CDOC changed suppliers— same drug, different color.)

"I wanna see the nurse pour it out in front of me." (All meds are pre-prepared in the medical suite. This is not like cherries jubilee prepared at your table.)

"How do I know what's in that stuff?" (You don't. Get over it.)

Still another group refuses to take their medication just to show us who's boss. I'm a *Calvin and Hobbes* fan, so the psychology is familiar. Here's an exchange I had with Stanton Porter, a diabetic car thief in CSP for assaulting a CO at Sterling Correctional Facility.

"The nurses tell me you're refusing your insulin."

Porter glares sullenly from his perch on the exam room gurney. "I'm not taking that shit."

"That's why we're getting together today. You're not taking your insulin because....?"

"I know what I need. You don't know shit."

"I know if you go off your insulin your blood sugar will shoot up to five hundred like it was before you started."

"What *you* say."

"So going blind, having your feet amputated, kissing your kidneys goodbye, having your nerves and blood vessels shot. That's the plan, right?"

Porter silently turns up the wattage on his menacing glower.

I threw in the towel. "OK. I guess you'll show me."

"Damn straight."

There are a few ways this will subsequently play out.

Porter will shortly go into a coma and get shipped to the hospital for resuscitation. There, everyone will wonder about the bozo doctor at the prison who doesn't know enough to prescribe insulin for a diabetic. He'll return to CSP and shape up since being dead is the ultimate 'dis. Or:

Porter will realize that being sick as a goat all the time is not worth the 'cred he's gaining by defying medical, and he'll send a kite promising to be a good boy if I'll just put him back on his meds. This, of course, requires him to admit he was mistaken, so it doesn't happen all that often. Or"

Porter, appreciating that he has made a tactical blunder in cutting off his own medications, will write a grievance citing "deliberate indifference" by medical, and me in particular, to his dire medical condition. This is a potentially face-saving ploy to "force" me to give him his constitutionally guaranteed medical care. By going the grievance route, a lengthy legal process, instead of just asking for his medication, he guarantees several more weeks of being without his meds. Or:

Porter will tough it out, slowly sinking into the morass of diabetic complications until he has some life-threatening event and I can legally intervene.

Non-compliance with medical programs is frequently curious, often nonsensical. Inmates work hard to get medication, and then refuse to take it. Laziness and defiance are often the reasons, but sometimes it's just deluded thinking. He's an example from Harvey Downey, a gang enforcer all the way from Detroit.

"Mr. Downey, I noticed you're not taking your blood pressure medicine. Why not?"

"My blood pressure's fine. I don't need that shit."

"Your blood pressure's fine *because* you've been taking the medicine. If you stop, it'll go up again."

"I guess I know my body better than you."

Hard to argue with that logic. Here's another one from Avery Franklin, a drug dealer from Durango.

"Mr. Franklin, you're not taking your seizure medicine. Why not?"

"I know my body. I work out. I keep it pure. I don't need that shit."

"You've had three seizures in the past month. What does your pure body tell you about that?"

"It don't say nothin' when I'm unconscious."

And in some terribly dark twisted way, this makes sense. Here's a conversation with Terry Fleming, a three-time loser at carjacking.

"Mr. Fleming, I see you're refusing your cholesterol medication. Why is that?"

"I was on Zocor on the street and it worked fine. Never any problems. Now you got me on this simvastatin shit and it don't work at all."

"Zocor *is* simvastatin. Same stuff. Zocor is just a brand name."

"Says you."

And so it goes.

Underlying all of this is the common attitude among CSP inmates that refusing medical care is somehow punishing me. It's as if they can picture me tossing and turning at night, sleepless with anxiety and re-morse at their undeserved medical misfortunes. Not.

I'm sure some of my colleagues fret and worry about their charges, but I seldom do. It's not that I'm indifferent to human suffering, and it's not that I think they "deserve it" for whatever crimes they committed to arrive here.

I've always looked at medicine as a team sport. If the patient doesn't want to be on the team, why should I? I can seldom bring about a sat-isfactory result all by myself, so I don't beat myself up when an inmate refuses to accept my advice. Ultimately, it's his problem, not mine.

W e have a club at CSP. It has no formal organization but is com-posed of inmates who like to swallow things. Anything. If they can get it past their teeth, it's gone.

These are sad people. Why they do this is a subject for someone else's doctoral thesis. I've talked extensively with my mental health colleagues about this phenomenon. After clearing away all the five-syllable words, I've concluded that they have no clue either.

It's hard to generalize beyond a certain point about who these peo-ple are. They tend to be individuals whose self-esteem and IQ are in negative digits. Some do it for attention, some because other inmates bully them into doing it, some because they like the trips to the hospital, some just want to get shipped out of CSP on any terms.

Are they crazy? The behavior is crazy, but outside of their propen-sity for swallowing foreign objects, they can seem very rational during an interview. Some express remorse and promise never to do it again (they always do, though). Some exude a certain amount of pride in their accomplishment, like the sword swallower at the circus. Some are defi-ant, just waiting for a chance to do it again.

It started out innocently enough with one inmate, Alfredo Garber, swallowing a package of colored pencils. Full length. Sharpened. I checked out the x-ray and sure enough, all twelve bundled up in a tight wad in his stomach with a few venturing into the small intestine. Too bad x-rays aren't in color. He'd be a rainbow.

Garber was lying on the exam table. He was laughing and joking, but quickly switched to being serious since he was "in excruciating pain."

"Just curious, Mr. Garber. What made you think that swallowing a box of colored pencils was a good idea?"

Garber tried to decide between giggling and grimacing. "I was hungry."

I took the comedy as a hopeful sign. Off he went to the ER, surgery, recovery, and back again to CSP. The proverbial bad penny. To the tune of $85,000 taxpayer dollars.

"Back so soon, Mr. Garber. Feeling better?"

"Feeling great. A little sore." He pointed to a line of sutures on his belly.

"Was this a learning experience?"

"Oh, yeah. I don't know why I did that. It was really stupid. I'll never do anything like that again."

Of course, Garber got another box of colored pencils and chugged them along with a few ballpoint pens before the check to the hospital cleared. Not to be outdone, another inmate, Elvis Foreman, broke off a metal sprinkler head in his cell and ate the whole thing. As a bonus, there's a flood to contend with. Another inmate ate some sporks, those utensils that combine a spoon and a fork. One swallowed an entire albuterol asthma inhaler.

It was a freaking epidemic. Anything not nailed down was ingested. Torn and knotted shirts, glass, D-rings, staples, nuts and bolts plus a stationery store full of pencils and pens.

I asked a few of these guys why they did it. Their answers seem to make sense to them at least: "Because I'm hungry." "Because I'm being sexually harassed." "Because I want to watch TV at the hospital." And best of all: "Because I want to cost you money." Graber was right about that last reason. Retrieving a pack of sharpened pencils and repairing multiple bowel perforations set the state back about $85,000, like I said. And that was just for one trip.

All told there were about a half dozen hard-core ingestors. I looked for the official guidelines on how to best handle this phenomenon, but there's not much in the medical literature. Most stuff is about kids swallowing coins. I consulted gastroenterologists and found as much elsewhere as I could. I wrote up a quick summary and now it's the unofficial CDOC guideline for how to handle ingested foreign bodies. I'm almost famous. I wonder if I could put this on my CV.

You might think that in a facility where each inmate is in his own cell with absolutely no contact with other prisoners, it should be a snap to keep things away from them that they might swallow. Cut off their pens, pencils, and other ingestible stuff. End of problem. They have a word for that concept: naïve.

First, there were the people who just didn't pay attention. A helpful staff officer passed the cell. "Hey, Sarge. I need a pen." Sure, pal, here you go.

Then there were the bleeding-heart liberals who believed, sincerely I think, that if an inmate gets a stern lecture and promises to be good, all is forgiven. I'll have to blow the whistle on my mental health colleagues for this one. "It's not humane that he doesn't even have a pen or pencil to write his ailing grandmother. He's promised he won't do it again." Here you go.

I have nothing but admiration for mental health workers' ability to put up with crates of bullshit and still display boundless optimism that inside everyone is good. But not at $85,000 a pop.

The other prisoners helped out too. It's a game. They ratlined pencils, pens, and other goodies to the ingestor's cell. Staff officers put dams in front of the doors so nothing could slide through the bottom crack. Didn't work. Why, I don't know, but it didn't.

The inmates above tied Care packages to string and flushed them down the toilet. The ingestor then fished the package out through his own toilet. Disgusting, but effective.

Foreign bodies were not confined to the intestinal tract. I have another group that liked to insert various objects up their penises. Everybody needs a hobby. I'm informed by the mental health folks that this is an auto-erotic practice that supposedly feels good. Right.

Last week I sent one member (no pun intended) to the ER after he pushed three pen tops up his penis into his bladder. Another went a few days earlier for lacerations from pushing parts of a spork up his butt. Still another declared a medical emergency because he couldn't remove the dental floss ligature he'd tied around his scrotum and it looked well on the way to amputation.

I'm going to have to take their word for the erotic ecstasy accompanying these maneuvers. Most are not first-timers, so they must know. Something in my Midwestern upbringing says this is just wrong. They sure didn't cover this in the sex-ed class I had in junior high.

These guys were not too far removed from the self-mutilators. These inmates periodically found something sharp enough to slice a chunk out of themselves. Arms and penises were the favored locations, but just about anywhere would do.

My first week on the job introduced me to Raymondo Cruz, a 32-year-old Hispanic forger with a strong history of childhood abuse according to my mental health colleagues. I was called up to the housing pod because the COs were afraid he was bleeding to death. Raymondo had smashed the unbreakable Lexan cover on his television set and sat on his bunk carving away at his forearm with a jagged piece.

When I arrived, the COs stood at the cell door trying to convince Raymondo to give up the shiv. I peeked through the narrow window and saw that while he was covered in blood, he'd just smeared it around from superficial cuts. "He's got to do better than that to really hurt himself," I said. Everybody relaxed except the SORT team, poised to do the forced cell extraction.

Some do a more thorough job. Brian McCloud, an ultraviolent Aryan supremacist, was a wizard at creating cutting implements and using them on himself. A few months ago he opened an eight-inch gash on his forearm, missing the major blood vessels but slicing open a huge chunk of muscle. He didn't want it fixed.

Ordinarily that would be the end of it, but the wound was so deep, it was too dangerous to leave it untreated. I insisted. He refused. He was a very big guy. And crazy.

It took a half-dozen burly COs piled on the gurney with McCloud spitting and screaming invectives, bucking like Colorado's namesake bronco. I thanked my stars for my surgical background and did the fastest wound closure of my career. McCloud was dragged off to Intake and went to work with his teeth ripping out my handiwork, thankfully not enough to get down to the vital stuff.

As if the wounds weren't bad enough, I have several inmates who stick foreign bodies or smear dirt or feces into their fresh injuries. One determined inmate saved chicken bones from his tray and stuck about fifty fragments into his legs.

Sadly, there's just not much to do for someone who is bent on self-destruction to this degree. Amazingly, they rarely get infections or suffer any permanent disability. They're immune to every bug on the planet.

You might think that the first thing to do when blood is hitting the ceiling is for medical personnel to rush in and save the day. Not so. Remember our emergency drills.

Keeping in mind that the inmates are here because they are the most dangerous and violent offenders in the prison system, they are not totally to be trusted. More than once a good Samaritan has rushed to the rescue only to be savagely attacked by the poor incapacitated crook. So there are rules of engagement.

When an inmate misbehaves, he is said to be non-compliant. There are two basic ways an inmate can be non-compliant in his cell. He can do something active, like throw his TV set into the wall, or something passive, like refusing to cuff up.

An inmate lying unresponsive on his bunk is considered non-compliant in this passive sense. He may be unconscious or even dead. He may be pissed off and purposely ignoring commands. Or he may be setting a trap.

Bottom line: If an inmate decides to throw a fit and slice himself up, he'd better pick a small blood vessel, because I'm not coming to the rescue anytime soon.

There are several ways that a prisoner can resist a CO. These, appropriately enough, are called levels of resistance.

I got my first practical dose of this while accompanying a nurse and a CO on medline for orientation. The procedure for taking medicine is regimented. The CO opens the tray slot, the nurse puts the medicine in a small paper cup on the opened tray, the inmate takes the pills, puts them in his mouth, takes some water from his cup and swallows. Simple. Except when they cheek the meds.

He can stuff the pills under his tongue, spit them back in the cup or drop them on the floor, slip them into a shirt sleeve or multiple other variations. If the nurse or CO spots something funny like the inmate turning away when he takes the pills, fumbling with the cup or acting like he's gargling the medicine, it's time for a mouth check and sometimes a cell search.

That's what happened with Dexter Knowles, a shifty wisp of a thief with more moves than Wheaton Van Lines. Knowles took the medication cup from the tray and suddenly coughed. Considerately, he covered his mouth with his hand.

"Knowles. Let's see your mouth. Now!" the CO barked.

Knowles hadn't had time to chug the water and complete the deception. He was in a jam. If a CO tells an inmate to open his mouth to check for medication, that's a lawful order. Knowles hesitated, so he got a warning. "Knowles, I'm giving you a lawful order to open your mouth." It sounds a little childish, but it gave Knowles fair warning that he was about to cross the line.

If Knowles wouldn't do it, that's non-compliance with a lawful order and he would be exhibiting passive resistance. Knowles wasn't doing anything, and that's the problem. He's supposed to do what he's told.

Knowles decided to brazen it out. He stuck his tongue out at the CO. "I already swallowed it." He turned and stomped back to his bunk. One of the pills rolled out of his sleeve onto the floor. Oops.

The CO called for reinforcements and ordered Knowles to come to the door and cuff up. Not caring for the alternative of getting a shower with OC spray, he slouched back to the door and cuffed up, grousing nonstop about his maltreatment.

The CO signaled for the control center to open Knowles' door and placed a hand on Knowles shoulder to move him out of the cell. Knowles pulled away from the CO, shrugging back into the cell. This is defensive resistance. He's not attacking the CO, but he's actively not cooperating.

Next on the list is active aggression. If Knowles should swat the CO's hand away, he's over that line. Close behind that is if Knowles started to fight or attack the CO. Then he's in the lethal force arena. At the top of the list is if Knowles tries to escape.

These levels of resistance are important because a CO is authorized to use force only one step above what Knowles is trying to pull. If Knowles pulls away from a grip, you can't shoot him, but you can go one level above his disobedience and take him down. Since the cameras are always on, everyone pays close attention to the level of force needed to resolve the situation.

As in war, the plan never survives first contact with the enemy. If a CO is in fear for his life, all bets are off. Knowles is going down quickly and not very gently. Once he's controlled, though, everyone has to back off. No extra punches or kicks. And that's pretty much how it happens unless Knowles really pisses somebody off. That usually happens when he fails to grasp the gravity of the situation and keeps trying to fight or bites somebody. On that day, Knowles backed off short of getting his ticket punched, but he was close.

TWENTY-TWO

THE PHARMACY

The pharmacy for the Cañon City prisons is run out of Pueblo, about an hour's drive to the east. To help with controlling costs, CDOC has a formulary, a group of "approved" medications. This helps reduce the need to carry multiple medications that do essentially the same thing. Your health plan has a formulary too. So far so good.

Because of the cost of newer drugs, you won't find many of the medications advertised on TV represented on the formulary. That's not necessarily a bad thing. If an older, cheaper medication works well, no problem.

But what happens when the older generic medications aren't doing the job? Then you have to go outside of the formulary for an alternative.

For most health plans, this means you pay a little more for the non-formulary or brand name medication. For CDOC it means the Non-Formulary Committee.

To get a non-formulary drug, instead of using the electronic medical record system, I had to fill out a paper form and fax it to the NF Committee. Included was not only a request for the drug I needed, but also my reasons for the request. Then they decided if they'd give it to me or not.

The committee is autocratic and proud of it. The system is based on the proposition that a pharmacist knows more about treating my patient than I do.

Imagine you're at your local Walgreen's handing the pharmacist a prescription from your doctor. The pharmacist frowns, turning the paper over in his hands as if it carries a vaguely unpleasant odor.

"I don't think you need this," he informs you.

"What do you mean, you don't think so," you say. "You're not my doctor. I didn't ask for your opinion."

"Let me see your chest x-ray," he demands. "And I'll need your latest liver function tests and a list of everyone in your family who has ever visited Armenia."

"You're a pharmacist," you protest. "Those things are none of your business. My medical records are between me and my doctor."

A suggestion of a smirk appears. "You want this," he waves the prescription slowly, tantalizingly in front of your nose, "you'll tell me whatever I want to know."

You snatch the prescription indignantly. "This is the last time you'll ever see me in this store!"

He flips a dismissive hand. "Fine. But just remember. I'm the only pharmacy in town."

Such was the procedure of the NF Committee. Yell, scream, kick. They didn't care. They didn't have to. I was talking to Ernestine of Lily Tomlin's Phone Company.

I'd never seen any system quite like it. I could freely prescribe dozens of formulary medications that could kill if not properly handled, but I had to justify an entire medical history to a committee to approve a Tylenol tablet.

If the Committee rejected my request, they supposedly give a sound reason, although any reason would do. I wanted some Tylenol. I got, "What back exercise program is this patient using?"

What difference did *that* make? And how did the pharmacy get to direct a physical therapy program? I didn't ask for their advice, but it came free of charge.

I couldn't just jot the answer to their question and email it. I had to go back and do the whole requisition with all the original information all over again and fax it back for another round.

It seemed they counted on my being so tired and fed up with the whole thing that I'd just let it drop. They were often right. I could only fight so many pointless battles in a day before the loopiness got to me.

I wasn't the only one singled out for this treatment. The mental health folks recently had a patient who had to take a medication by court order. Being a good CSP inmate, he refused to take the pill.

Okay, big boy. We gotta give you a different medicine by injection then. But the NF Committee insisted that the mental health guys didn't need the injectable form of the second medicine. You can give him a pill. So now the nurses get to scratch their heads about how they're going to give a pill to someone who won't take a pill, or how they can get the prescribed medication from a pharmacy that won't dispense it.

Just in case you think I was being too rough on my pharmacy colleagues, I got a rejection once when I requested a bar of soap. The reason? I hadn't specified directions for use. I should have referred them to their mothers.

CDOC has "clinical guidelines" specifying how certain diseases should be handled. One of these covers asthma. Specifically it covers what to do if an inmate uses his Albuterol inhaler, a quick-acting "rescue" medication, more than a couple of times per week. In that case it's best to add a second medicine to prevent the spells from happening in the first place.

The first one to try, and (gasp!) the cheapest is drug A. After a fair trial of A, if things aren't getting better, the guidelines say to proceed to drug B. Sounds reasonable.

Inmate Smith isn't getting any better on drug A. He's sucking Albuterol like a leech in a blood bank. In goes the request to the NF Committee for drug B, stating that A isn't working.

Back comes the denial.

- Where are the spirometry results? (We don't have a spirometer.)
- How do you know the inmate really took drug A? (I don't. Just because the medical records show he took a full inhaler and gave back an empty one is no sign he actually used it. He probably just spritzed it on his salad.)
- Where are the physical examination findings? (Gee, I must have forgotten to do that. Isn't it the pharmacist's job to listen to the lungs?)
- Have you ever been a member of the John Birch Society? (Just kidding about this one. I think.)

Bottom line: No drug B for Smith. We're stuck with Drug A that the CDOC guidelines say I shouldn't use because it isn't working. I should use Drug B that I can't get. Y'all come back real soon.

I've never understood a system that encouraged a pharmacy committee to overrule an on-site physician's order, and which directed the medical care of a patient they'd never seen and for whom they accepted no responsibility. I took my protests up the chain of command and was told as gently as possible to shut the fuck up.

My protestations, however, didn't go unnoticed. Often in life the squeaky wheel gets the grease. In the case of the pharmacy, the squeaky wheel got the denials.

I saw one of the members of the NF Committee at a meeting last month. I brought up my frustration in trying to get even routine prescriptions approved. He said, with a straight face, that often my requests were denied "for personal reasons." When I asked what that meant, he just smiled.

I wouldn't mind this territorial pissing so much except people—my patients—get hurt. No matter how I personally felt about an inmate and what brought him to that sorry state, as a physician I was bound to do the absolute best I can for him.

That my pharmaceutical colleagues seemed to do their damnedest to frustrate that goal was beyond offensive. I could only guess at their motives. Cost savings for the State? Unlikely. Helping the feebleminded physicians pick the right medicine? Please. Power? Now you're talking!

To me, it violated the oath I took when I got my medical degree. I realize that sounds all high and mighty, but it's the way I feel. I was the guy sitting in front of another human being, talking with him, examining him, and using all my skill, experience, and intuition to come up with the right diagnosis and treatment plan. It was my responsibility for the whole thing.

A pharmacist is a highly skilled professional, but she's not an M.D. Not by a long shot. She had never seen the patient, nor was she qualified to do so. She accepted no responsibility for his care other than correctly filling the physician's prescription. So why was this system set up for a pharmacist to overrule a physician, even if the pharmacist hid behind a committee? Can you tell this was a burr under my saddle?

I thought other physicians at CDOC might feel the same way, so I approached several of them early on in my corrections career to get their take on this. It was unanimous. They knew the system sucked, but they didn't want to get involved in correcting it. Their advice: Just put in your hours, go home, and forget about it. Probably good advice from their points of view, but a huge and continuing discouragement for me.

TWENTY-THREE

ADMINISTRATION

Life as a prison doctor is not all just fun and games with the pharmacy. From time to time, prisons need to demonstrate what a good job they are doing. In outside industry a certification procedure called ISO 9000 gives companies a gold star for good work. Prisons use the American Corrections Association review to demonstrate their compliance in following the rules and regulations.

Christa, one of the nursing supervisors, came to me with a look of confused consternation: "I needed to use this chart for an ACA review, but I can't because the inmate wasn't scheduled for a follow-up exam when he returned from the infirmary."

"But I just saw him. I just did the exam."

"Yes, but there wasn't an order in the chart to do it."

"You mean I didn't write an order to myself to do the exam that I just did?"

"Right."

"So if I write myself an order to do what I've already done, you can do your review?"

"I don't know. I think you've got to write the order first, then do the exam, then I can do the review."

"I could say 'I forgot,' and pre-date the order."

"I think the computer time stamps it."

"What if I didn't use the computer? What if the computer was down when I went to write the order?"

"It was?"

"You bet. Hang on a second." (turning and scribbling) "Wow! Here it is!"

"What?"

"The order. Right here. It was on my desk the whole time. See? Dated yesterday."

"Gosh, it was lucky you found it."

"Sometimes I just amaze myself."

When I restarted my medical career as a general practitioner I found salvation on the internet. There was information everywhere, most of it for free. Drug databases, medical forums—it was marvelous. If I had these kinds of resources in medical school, I could have spent a lot more time drinking and less time poring through twenty-pound texts.

Even with the glacial-paced CDOC computer network, finding information was orders of magnitude faster and more current than pawing through old textbooks. CDOC subscribed to a medical über-database that supplied data about diseases I didn't even know existed. It was fantastic.

If things are going well, someone will fix it. In this case, the CDOC administration thought it would be a good idea to shut off internet access to all medical providers. They reasoned if they could cut out the medical pukes there would be more bandwidth for the administrators. I knew they pulled this stuff in China all the time, but apparently Colorado was now added to the information no-fly zone.

This development was particularly important to me since I wasn't smart enough to practice without supplemental information. I sent an email to the Big Cheese pointing out that the expensive medical database was no longer available to anyone except administrative staff and clerks. If I wanted a refresher on treating ulcerative colitis, I'd have to ask the warden's secretary to look it up for me.

Apparently they hadn't thought of that. Time passed. The fullness of the seasons rotated. I got an email that declared medical providers could now access the medical database, but nothing else on the internet. As I learned at the next provider meeting, everything else on the internet was just time-wasting garbage and porn.

Like Watergate and The Grassy Knoll, I probably will never know the real story behind the Great Information Blackout. My theory is that it spontaneously arose from a bottle of peppermint schnapps at an administrative retreat. As in all things that seemed like A Good Idea at the Time, when the furor over the consequences broke, everyone that had anything to do with it was running for the bunkers and lobbing grenades at subordinates.

As dandelions regenerate after mowing the lawn, the next generation of administrators will unscrew a pint of Jagermeister and say, "Hey, why don't we put internet service into the medical clinics? It's damn near free, and we could stop paying for this stupid database thing they're using now." Mark my words.

———

Tricky Dick Nixon. Teflon Ronald Reagan. Slick Willie Clinton. Evasion, buck passing and general lack of candor are clichés in politics. Standing back and dispassionately observing the weasel behavior rampant in bureaucracies such as CDOC, I'll have to admit to a grudging admiration.

It takes talent to avoid a straight answer. Within limits, the truth is often the easiest response to a direct question. Consider one of my recent queries to administration: "What's the reason you turned off my internet access?" The straightforward answer might run something like, "No reason. I just felt like screwing with you."

A seasoned bureaucrat would never contemplate such a response. First rule: Deny any knowledge of the subject. "Internet? Never heard of it."

The advantages of this approach are not only its simplicity but also its stunning stupidity. This creates a disconnect, shifting the focus from the problem into the abstract world of basic concepts. It's as if I mistakenly used a big word that a child couldn't understand, forcing me to back up and define terms.

I could try calling, but the bureaucrat or his/her secretary would hang up. Emails or voicemails were automatically greeted with, "Director Blub is away from her throne today. Please leave a message and press the star key to delete it."

Persistence is the enemy of the CDOC bureaucrat. When I got through again, explaining what the internet is and why it might be important, the director fell back to the Second Rule: Blame it on someone else.

"Internet service is out? You should contact BT (Business Technologies) about that." Click.

Naturally, BT was the first stop in the diagnostic chain, long before I considered slogging to the troll cave of administration. BT admitted they had turned off the service at the request of administration, but had no idea why. The only certainty was that it was not a technical problem.

When I confronted the director with her duplicity, it was time for the Third Rule: Conduct a study.

"Internet service is out? We'll review that."

"Review what? BT says you're the one who told them to turn it off. What was the reason?"

The pressure was on. Creativity came to the fore in the form of the Fourth Rule: Pass the Buck. Smooth as a baton in an Olympic relay, the reply came to the director's lips. "It's not up to me. Richelle said to do it."

It's generally considered poor bureaucratic form to actually name the responsible person. The correct response would have been, "It's not up to me. I'm just passing on orders from upper administration." See how much better? Obstructive, ignorant and anonymous. A CDOC trifecta.

She could have obscured the true information even more if she quoted a committee. Something along the lines of, "I'm just implementing the policy of the CDOC Information Access Guidelines Committee." Then, like the Nazis, she's only following orders.

With this scrap of information, I sensed victory. I had the perpetrator's name and a reluctant witness. I pressed my advantage. "I'm sure Richelle must have had a good reason. What was it?"

"You'd have to ask her."

"Great. I'll tell her you ratted her out. How do you spell your last name? Is that moron with one 'r' or two?" Click.

Even though this might appear a defeat for the bureaucrat, consider that she succeeded in consuming piles of my time to no real benefit. I was no closer to getting the requested answer, let alone correcting the problem.

Now with the bone in my teeth I quested through the hallowed halls and actually ran Richelle to ground. Only two paths were open to her. The first involved "taking the Fifth," which invokes the Fifth Rule: Blame the subordinate.

This was rarely used, as it meant sacrificing a minion for no benefit other than immediate gratification. The possibility also lurked that the skewered subordinate who knows where the skeletons are buried, might, like a scalded hyena, retaliate in the future.

The safer and more common path was to recycle to the First Rule: Deny all knowledge, just like *Mission Impossible.*

Pleading ignorance is dangerously close to the truth for any bureaucrat, but at these exalted levels, directors can dance the razor's edge of veracity like Nijinsky. Continual deflection rather than outright opposition is the name of the game. This brings the entire process full circle, like Groundhog Day, leaving me no option but to start the process over again with a new player. Bottom line: No answers, no internet.

Circling the black hole of CDOC administration, where no light escapes and all information is annihilated, I wonder what manner of beings inhabit such a space. Weird, sure, but are they, as Stephen Hawking would have us believe, truly malevolent? Perhaps they operate in some parallel universe, not really in touch with our world, but creating random cataclysms for their own unfathomable reasons. Perhaps there are no sentient beings behind the curtain at all.

Alan Turing was an English mathematician and logic expert. In 1950 he proposed his famous test of whether a machine could be considered intelligent. He proposed that if an observer carried on a natural language conversation with two unseen entities, one a human and one a computer and could not tell which was which, this was a test for intelligence in the machine.

I'm feeling more generous than Turing, stacking the deck in favor of the humans. My setup would be to have the observer carry on a natural language conversation with two unseen entities, one a CDOC administrator and one a block of lime Jell-O.

I feel strongly that the observer would not be able to tell the difference, thus establishing edible gelatin as fit for government service. Some may scoff, but this seems to fit the observable facts better than any other theory. Until I can get Hawking on the phone, I'm going with it.

TWENTY-FOUR

OUTTA HERE—EXECUTIONS, ESCAPES, SUICIDES AND PAROLE

Everyone gets out of jail eventually. Some die of natural causes, some killed by their fellow inmates, but most "kill their number" and get paroled. Some go out in a more public way.

Everyone loves a good execution. Until 1933, executions in Colorado were by hanging. Forty-five convicts met their end this way. Always progressive, Colorado came up with a hanging machine that supposedly eliminated the danger of a rope breaking or an agonizing death by strangulation. Even better, it didn't require the services of a hangman.

With this device, the condemned man stepped on a floor plate, triggering a noose that jerked him three feet into the air. In theory this would immediately break his neck. In theory.

In actual practice the machine turned out to be a disappointment, especially for the user, with most of the victims dying a slow death by strangulation. In one case the condemned dangled for twenty-four minutes before finally succumbing. Improvements were needed, and technology answered the call with the gas chamber.

The gas chamber was installed at Territorial Prison in 1934, ultimately claiming thirty-two lives before being replaced by lethal injection. The first gas chamber was a three-seater personally designed by

Warden Roy Best and nicknamed "Roy's Penthouse" due to its perch on the hill behind the prison. There was never a triple execution, but in 1933 the two Pacheco brothers were executed together for multiple murders. That original gas chamber lives on today in the Museum of Colorado Prisons in Cañon City.

There have been no executions since the mid-1960s with the exception of Gary Lee Davis, a murderer and rapist who was executed in 1997 by lethal injection. Currently there are two inmates on Colorado's death row, both multiple murderers.

I've never seen an execution, nor do I want to, but the actual procedure is chillingly clinical. It's very much like you've seen on TV with the last meal, the priest, the last-minute phone hookup, the witnesses and the protesters.

———

Just before the sally port into E-Pod there's a brown metal door marked "Hearings." It looks like dozens of others that lead to offices or storage areas. But this one leads to Room G217, the execution room.

To the left are showers and restrooms for men and women. To the right are two doors. One leads to a conference room with tables and chairs for the witnesses. In the day-to-day operation of the prison this is often used as a regular conference room for meetings. In the end wall of the witness room is a large glass window facing onto G217.

G217 is sterile and windowless with a holding cell, a chair, and a medical examination table with Velcro straps.

The Hippocratic Oath excludes medical personnel from participating in any way with the actual execution. The execution team is selected from a pool of volunteers who often have experience as EMTs or military medics. All that's really required is the skill to start an IV and the willingness to do it.

The injection is done remotely with a dummy setup so a volunteer doesn't know if he actually did the injection. Sometimes men volunteer for a subsequent execution, but once is usually more than enough.

Preparation for an execution may extend out for a year. Staff education meetings specify what the process entails, provide training for the volunteer team, and prepare for the inevitable PR storm. It's all carefully choreographed and timed with provision for everything from the psychological counseling of staff to how the body is moved through the prison to the waiting hearse. Regardless of how you might feel about capital punishment, the whole process is very corporate and cold-blooded.

When I first came to CSP there was one inmate on the launching pad, Nathan Dunlap. Initially, he robbed a Burger King at gunpoint where he had been employed. That time he just took the money.

On December 14, 1993, at the age of nineteen, he shot five employees of a Chuck E Cheese restaurant where he had previously been fired. Four died but one, though shot in the face, escaped to later identify Dunlap as the assailant.

Like many CSP inmates, Dunlap gave vague and contradictory reasons for the crime. One time it was seeking revenge against the company. Another it was to get money to pay parking tickets. None of it made any sense.

He was sentenced to death in May of 1996 and was sent to CSP to await execution. He's still waiting as I write this in 2013.

He's been on two hunger strikes but Colorado won't permit suicide, even on death row. That brought me into the picture since I'm entrusted with keeping his health tiptop. He slouched into the exam room in shackles, trailing two COs in his wake. A contemptuous sneer distorted a boyish face.

Dunlap is careless, arrogant, and completely indifferent to the harm he caused. Unfortunately, he's young and healthy, so we've got a long way to go with this process.

I've attended staff meetings over the past three years concerning the execution process, but it seems that it's never really going to happen. It's not that I'm anxious to see anyone killed, but it does seem ludicrous to sentence someone to death and then still be sitting around in limbo almost two decades later.

J ail breaks are the stuff of legend. When I was being drilled at the training academy in how to behave as a hostage, I wondered just how often escapes happen. Fairly often, as it turns out.

In any given year about one-half of one percent of the total prison population escapes or goes AWOL from state institutions. That's thousands of prisoners. Most escapes are not the sophisticated, carefully planned operations of the movies. The vast majority are "walk-aways" from minimum security facilities. Almost all are quickly recaptured.

You have to wonder about the mentality of these low-time escapees. Most are getting close to parole or release. The penalty for escape can tack another eight years onto their expiring terms. Who's doing the math here?

The odds are stacked against escapees. Without money and transportation, they usually don't have a support structure on the outside except for what they can mooch from family and friends. The cops know this and are waiting when they make contact.

It's not always safe for the pursuers either. The first prison employee killed in the line of duty was mistakenly shot by a sheriff's posse in 1899 while guarding a bridge escape route. At the time of the shooting the posse didn't know that the escaped convict had already been apprehended and returned to the prison.

The first big escape from Colorado State Penitentiary occurred in 1874 with eight desperados fleeing through Cañon City with guns and knives. This assault on the community convinced the citizens that a sole nighttime guard was insufficient security. They voted to construct a wall around the prison compound, a feature it lacked before then.

Things started getting serious when a 1929 escape attempt turned into a riot that destroyed major parts of the prison. In the 1930s bloodhounds were kept at the prison to track down escapees. Without a thought to the irony, the prison officials put prisoners in charge of training and handling the dogs.

Escape attempts from the more secure modern prisons grab the headlines. In 1989, two men escaped the Arkansas Valley Correctional

Facility in Ordway, Colorado by helicopter. Even these inventive types were back in prison the next day.

Fremont in Cañon City is a medium-security facility just around the bend from CSP. A prisoner walked away from a summer work detail at Fremont and ran through a cornfield down to the Arkansas River. It got dark and the mosquitoes started to eat him alive. He was terrified of getting West Nile fever from the bugs, so he ran to the highway and flagged down a patrol car to take him back to the prison.

Another Fremont escape was almost accomplished by two men who made cardboard shields that looked like rocks. They slowly backed their way across the property and got under the first of two fences surrounding the prison. A random head count foiled the plot before they could get past the second.

Centennial, my second prison home in Cañon City, was the old Colorado supermax. Nonetheless, a prisoner climbed out of an outdoor recreation cage, got on top of the two-story building and jumped to freedom. Unfortunately, he broke his leg on landing. He called to the COs inside to come get him.

Even impregnable CSP has had an escape of sorts. Due to a mix-up in paperwork, a lifer was given a bus ticket, a hundred bucks, and released. He couldn't resist bragging about his escape to his old friends at CSP. His calls from Pennsylvania were monitored and traced. Back to the slammer.

Sterling Correctional Facility, the site of the most recent escape, is located about 120 miles northeast of Denver. It's the largest of the CDOC facilities with over 2500 inmates.

The inmate, Douglas Alward, was jailed in 1980 for attempted murder. He fashioned a ladder from copper pipe he'd accumulated in his trustee job as a plumber and got past three (count 'em) twelve- to fifteen-foot perimeter fences to escape.

Just getting out of his cell should have been impossible, as all the windows were riveted shut the previous year. But who was trusted to do the riveting? Alward.

The inner fence was a "shaker" fence, which sets off an alarm if disturbed. I wondered how you could put a ladder against a fence without touching it, but apparently the winds around Sterling can be pretty fierce and the sensitivity was likely turned down. Alward almost lost it there when the ladder broke when he was at the top, entangling him in the razor wire for a time. "There's a good reason for calling it razor wire," Alward said.

The second fence was a "stun-lethal" fence which gives you a stunning shock the first time you touch it and a lethal one the second time. He used a shower curtain and cardboard to slide under this one without touching the wires.

The third fence, topped with ordinary barbed wire would have been a breeze without any special electronics associated with it. He scrambled over and out. Alward said the entire escape took less than forty seconds.

The inmate was on foot for a couple of days, tracked not only by prison personnel, but also the Colorado State Police and the FBI. He was finally located near the tiny town of Yuma, Colorado nearly fifty miles from the prison.

Alward got a handgun from the owner of a mobile home and held a woman hostage for several hours. During that time he had her wait in the bathroom facing away from him while he took a shower and brushed his teeth.

Surrounded by law enforcement personnel, Alward said, "Well, I guess this is it." Instead of a desperate shootout, he released his hostage and walked out the back door of the trailer, surrendering without a fight. So much for Hollywood.

Although Alward was the first person to escape from Sterling, he had escaped six times from other prison facilities. Even though he proved to be a great escape artist, his timing was poor. His Sterling escape was in August of 2010. He was up for parole in October.

Territorial, being the oldest of the Colorado prisons, also hosts the most escapes. Some border on the bizarre. One involved a fifteen-year-old boy, Jimmy, sentenced to life for the murder of his mother and father.

There was an old irrigation canal that originally ran in front of the prison buildings, but later was enclosed within the walls as the prison expanded. It flowed in the west wall, ran through the central portion of the prison and out the east wall to Cañon City. About fifteen feet wide and four feet deep, it not only served as a potential escape route, but also for attempts to float contraband into the prison from outside.

Jimmy fabricated a camouflaged frogman outfit complete with a snorkel made from electrical conduit. The enterprising aquanaut, outfitted with a hacksaw and extra blades, sawed through his cell bars, which faced outside next to the canal, slipped into the water during an eleven p.m. shift change and dragged himself against the current to two rows of upright two-inch steel bars blocking his exit.

He was working on sawing through the final bar when the current tore away his snorkel and he was forced to surface right next to the night patrol. Close, but no cigar.

Another Territorial almost-escape occurred in 1970 on the date of the annual Cañon City Blossom Festival. Two condemned murderers were in an interior exercise yard. One boosted the other onto the roof by standing on a water faucet. The first man then lowered his leg for the second to climb after him. The two scampered across the roofs of the cellblock and were almost to the outside wall when they were spotted by tower guards.

Both were gunned down with shotguns from the towers and fell dead outside the wall next to a high school band waiting to enter the parade. Everyone thought it was some kind of performance and applauded.

We haven't had a movie-style riot at CSP, but I did manage to get the next best thing when I received two inmates at CSP from the minimum-restricted facility at Cheyenne Mountain Re-entry Center (CMRC). What's up with this?

It seems these guys had about a week to go before release and decided they didn't want to do the rehab programs anymore. They staged a sit-in and encouraged the other inmates to join them. In CDOC that's called "facility disruption." In lay terms, it's the same as inciting a riot. Bam! Two years at CSP. Ya gotta wonder.

Let's face it. Looking at a lengthy stay in a maximum-security prison can be depressing. It's fairly common for inmates to want to cut out early via suicide.

Most suicide attempts at CSP are unsuccessful due to lack of opportunity and materials. In prison you have to get creative to kill yourself.

The most common method is strangulation. It's why CSP doesn't have pipes or bedposts to hang from. No shoelaces or belts either. At CSP II, the new improved supermax, they've installed clothes hooks that collapse under any significant weight. I think I've got some of those in my house.

Nonetheless, there are always points of attachment that can be found for homemade nooses made from clothing or bedding. If a noose can't be made to work, some will try strangulation by tightening ligatures around the neck with a twisting pencil for leverage, cutting off circulation if not the airway.

Asphyxiation with plastic bags over the head or stuffing objects into the nose and mouth to occlude the airway is a less-favored method, but gruesomely effective.

Drugs are the next most common suicide modalities. Inmates may accumulate toxic doses of prescription medication either through hoarding their own medicines or obtaining them from other prisoners.

Prisoners are ignorant concerning how much of a particular agent it takes to do real damage or if a particular drug will cause death in overdose at all. Frequently they try to cover all the bases by taking a cocktail of multiple drugs. Although it presents a confusing clinical picture to those of us on the receiving end in the emergency room, they often take medication with conflicting effects. Taking uppers and downers leaves you somewhere in the middle with only an upset stomach.

Usually drug overdose is more of a recreational embarrassment rather than a suicide attempt. A little too much happy juice earns the celebrant a dose of Narcan, a narcotic antagonist, to spoil the fun. Most get a trip to the ER and an elephant of a hangover.

Self-inflicted wounds are pretty common. We've got lots of "cutters" who like to slice themselves up when they get the chance. Pieces of a smashed "unbreakable" TV shell, a sharp piece of metal or glass contraband, or just their own teeth are the usual instruments of destruction. The cutters seldom do more than lacerate their skin, but a few have found an artery. My conservative friends have suggested I give classes on how to do it right.

Falls are a popular means of prison exit, if the inmate has access to heights. Nobody has taken a dive off a second story tier at CSP to my knowledge, but plenty have taken to repeatedly bashing their heads into the cement walls. We have had a few that tried suicide by diving off their beds onto the concrete floor, but no fatalities yet. Ouch!

The hunger strikers are almost always out to protest some perceived injustice and don't really contemplate carrying their strikes to death. In any case, it's a pretty pokey way to kill yourself. Since the medical staff is well aware of their state of health as the strike progresses, it's almost impossible for the inmate to exit via this strategy.

Our crew of "ingestors," those pathetic people who swallow foreign objects, seem to mostly do this to get attention or for a trip to the hospital. None seem bent on suicide, although their activities could easily end up that way.

All these things bring up the question of why inmates commit suicide in the first place and how it can be prevented. Some retribution-minded individuals argue that we shouldn't prevent it. "Let the bastards kill themselves!" While it's a point of view I can appreciate, as a physician I can't go there. But how can you motivate prisoners, particularly lifers, to want to continue living in an environment that makes them want to die?

———

M ary Belle Harris, the first female warden of a US federal prison said, "We must always remember that the doors of prisons swing both ways." Sad but true, most of the guys in prison will get out. As heinous as the crime may be, when the sentence is up, the inmate becomes a civilian again.

Before the Mandatory Release Date (MRD), when the official sentence has run out, there are opportunities for most inmates to earn a get-out-of-jail-free card—parole.

Some don't want parole. Inmates with no ties to the community, no family or friends on the outside, often waive the right to a parole hearing so they can stay where they feel safe and secure. Even those whose prison term is up may commit further infractions so their stay can be extended indefinitely. Compared to being homeless, a warm place to sleep and three squares a day looks pretty good.

Also the friendships an inmate makes, especially in a general population prison, can be like the friends you make in school or the military. A free, sort-of-comfy home surrounded by your buds. What could be better? For the rest, there is the possibility of parole.

Except for the most serious felonies with a minimum sentence of life imprisonment, all inmates qualify for consideration of parole once they have served half of their sentences. If an inmate earns the maximum allowable "good time," the earliest parole date works out to 38 percent of the sentence.

Before an inmate can be released from a CDOC facility, he has to have a parole plan in place that details where he will live and work and who will be responsible for him on release.

A lot goes into a parole hearing. The parole board considers not only the nature of the inmate's crime, but also prior offenses and his behavior in prison, including rehabilitation programs.

Medical and psychological evaluations also play a part, although my medical opinion seldom has much effect that I can see. I always thought it was a seat-of-the-pants kind of decision as to whether the inmate made a good presentation to the board, but not so. It gets complicated, with points awarded or deducted for a multitude of factors.

The state's current budget crunch puts pressure on the board to parole inmates that in other economic times would be retained in prison. The percentage of persons sent to prison has grown ten times more than the population growth of the state, so overcrowding also cries out for shorter sentences and early paroles.

The inmate's troubles don't end by being paroled. Unless he has some kind of support structure helping with a place to live, a job, and at least a little financial help, it's very easy to slide back into what he knows best—crime. Almost 30 percent of prison admissions are for parole violations.

TWENTY-FIVE

TERRITORIAL, COLORADO'S
FIRST PRISON

The western United States of the 1800s fostered its own brand of lawlessness, and it wasn't long before the various hell-raisers, thieves, and murderers of the region needed a more permanent home than the local jail.

Territorial Correctional Facility, constructed in 1871 on the opposite side of Cañon City from present-day CSP, was the original Colorado State Penitentiary. The two-story, forty-two cell prison contained tiers of fourteen cells and one bathroom with an iron bathtub. Each iron cell was secured with a "first quality" lock.

As the years demanded expansion of the prison, inmate labor enlarged it by quarrying stone from the walls of a towering bluff behind the site. The only part of Territorial not surviving to modern times is the original forty-two-cell prison, which was destroyed in a 1929 riot.

The first Territorial prisoner arrived in January 1871—John Shepler, a German incarcerated for larceny. Wasting little time, the first escape came in December of that year. It was a little easier then since the prison lacked a surrounding wall until four years later.

The original penitentiary was co-ed, with the first female prisoner admitted in 1873 for manslaughter. Both sexes were housed in the same unit, separated only by bars. It wasn't until 1935 that a separate women's prison was built. It served until 1968 when a new women's facility was constructed on the east side of the city. The original women's prison building now serves as the Museum of Colorado Prisons.

Strange, haunted stories are told of the original women's prison. An inmate named Fran in cell eighteen kept a parakeet. After her death, the inmates in cells seventeen and nineteen kept hearing the bird and the sounds of moving furniture and conversation coming from eighteen.

The warden, Wayne Patterson, gave little credence to the reports. He returned late one evening to the old building after the inmates had been moved to the new women's prison. He later wrote, "I heard such a plethora of noises: steam lines banging, the walls cracking and popping, lights coming on before I hit a switch. There were sounds like women's voices and furniture being moved across the floor in part of the tier. I was glad to get out and go home."

Another story in the old women's prison concerned an inmate who had stabbed another woman in the doorway to the kitchen. A blood-stain continued to appear despite extensive scrubbing.

The tales continue today among prison museum volunteers with no prior knowledge of the hauntings. They still report seeing the blood-stains appear and hearing furniture moving.

The warden's family lived in a house inside the prison walls with the deputy warden living in a house on the outside of the east wall. This arrangement allowed for leadership to always be available in an emergency. Amazingly, prisoners drove the warden's children to school. I'm pretty sure that wouldn't happen now.

Prison administrators couldn't let all that free labor go to waste. The prison quickly added shoemaking, tailoring, blacksmithing, and carpentry shops as well as road work and brick making crews. There were even cooperative efforts with private contractors. In 1878 a boot and shoe company paid the prison fifty cents daily for the services of seventy convicts working nine and a half hours per day.

Inmates built many of the major Colorado highways. U.S. Highway 50, which snakes through the canyons linking Cañon City with Salida, was built primarily with inmate labor. Likewise the road to the top of the scenic Royal Gorge was a prison project.

An old picture of a work gang from CSP shows some of the men wearing dresses. I later learned that homosexual inmates were forced to wear women's clothing even on work crews.

I blundered into the most terrifying construction one day on my lunch break. Soon after beginning my CSP employment, I would take my brown bag lunch out to a park just to get out of the omnipresent cement tomb. I tried different spots to see a little of the surrounding country and parked one sunny afternoon under a sign that proclaimed, "Sky-Line Drive."

I still had a little time after eating, so I drove up the single-lane road to see if there was a view. There was.

Sky-Line Drive runs along the apex of a ridge just to the west of town. Sounds pretty, doesn't it? As I climbed the back of the ridge, I passed several "One Way Only" signs. The sides of the road closed in tighter and tighter. I topped out eight hundred feet above the valley floor, perpendicular walls plunging down both sides, toward town on my left and U.S. 50 on my right.

The road squeezed to a tiny single track atop a knife-edged ridge. No turnarounds. A narrow black ribbon undulated along dips and crests into the distance, mocking my suddenly sweating palms. The wind ripped across the ridge, rocking the car. Jesus H. Christ! What is this place?

If a car could creep on hands and knees, that's what I did for the next half hour. I know I oozed south several miles along that asphalt, but my eyes were glued to the road, never straying to the odometer. Finally, I reached a hairpin turn to the left and inched down the slope into a back neighborhood of Cañon City. I kissed the ground.

Later, I learned that the inmates of Territorial Prison constructed Sky-Line Drive that way on purpose as a scenic attraction. Their way of getting even, I suppose. Incredibly, it was originally a two-lane gravel road perched on the limestone ridge. I've seen old pictures of people up there in horse-drawn carts. That would be much better. With a horse, you can close your eyes.

I n the early 1900s the prison hired a music teacher and formed a band. It grew to about fifty members by 1920 and gave regular concerts during the summer for the Cañon City residents, playing from the second-story porch of the old administration building.

The citizens could easily reach the venue, as the main street of Cañon City ran in front of the prison. Anyone on the street could walk right into the prison, although a guard was posted to keep out the merely curious. It's still that way today with people walking up to the main gate looking for a tour.

The prison band played in the annual Music and Blossom Parade down the main street of Cañon City. The marching band belted out Sousa tunes while armed guards patrolled back and forth on foot and horseback beside the procession.

For those not musically inclined, the prison had a "grudge pit" next to the administration building. Prisoners who had a beef could make an appointment for the pit. On Saturday mornings they could meet and fight it out before a gallery of guards and other prisoners. With Sousa tunes in the background.

T he 1920s were an interesting time for another Cañon City organization, the Ku Klux Klan. The Klan was a national movement at that time, yet it was in Colorado that it achieved its greatest political success. Colorado's progressive leanings caused it to be the only Klan state with a women's auxiliary.

Although the Klan of the '50s and '60s was a violent hate group predominantly in the southern United States, the 1920s Klan was a different animal. This Klan was primarily a social fad inspired by Thomas Dixon's racist novel *The Clansmen,* and the resulting Hollywood movie, D. W. Griffith's *The Birth of a Nation.*

The Klan fancied itself a heroic organization of nightriders defending the virtue of womanhood. In Colorado it played out more as a political organization bent on promoting "100% Americanism" and opposing lawlessness, especially the skirting of Prohibition laws.

The history of the Klan in Colorado is a fascinating tale of political ambition and the hucksterism of an Atlanta traveling salesman, Imperial Wizard William Joseph Simmons. The Klan recruited many prominent individuals throughout the state and infiltrated much of the government.

The governor was a Klansman. The mayor of Denver was elected with Klan support, as was a U.S. senator and several state legislators. Klan members occupied the majority of the seats in the state House of Representatives. All over the state, offices from dog catcher to sheriff to mayor were dominated by the Klan.

In Cañon City, the Klan decided to take over administration of the prison. Warden Tynan learned of the Klan plot, locked the gates to the prison, and stationed a machine gun at the entrance. He carefully screened anyone applying for admission and rooted out Klan members from his staff of officers, assigning them to jobs outside the prison walls.

Finally, a coalition of both Republicans and Democrats united in 1928 and voted out the Klan members. For all its efforts to pass discriminatory legislation during its brief tenure, the Klan-dominated legislature only managed to pass two bills. One required schools to fly the American flag. The other made owning a still for brewing liquor a felony. The prison was saved.

Roy Phelix Best took over as warden of Colorado State Penitentiary in 1932 at one of the lowest points of its history. He was tasked with rebuilding the entire physical plant of the prison, which suffered massive destruction in the riot of 1929. Roy was an odd, but effective choice for the job.

Without any administrative skills or real training in penology, Roy nevertheless carved a flamboyant place in Territorial's history. His detractors liked to say he would have made a better mafia boss than a warden.

A broncobuster in his youth, he ran a Wild West show in New York into bankruptcy, having to hitchhike back to Colorado. Boone Best, Roy's father, was a state legislator and a friend of Governor William Adams. Adams appointed Boone as warden of the prison and gave Roy a job as his driver. When Boone was killed in a car-train collision, Roy inherited his father's job in 1932.

Best, Stetson cocked back on his round head and cigar clamped firmly in his teeth, loved to stroll the prison yard accompanied by his two Dobermans, Chris and Ike. He was a great believer in putting the prisoners to work, with the proceeds used to reduce the cost of their confinement. It worked. He dropped the cost of feeding a prisoner to only a dime a day.

He was big on organization. A chain-of-command chart from his era showed the physician on the same level as the dairy officer and cattle buyer. At least the doctor made it above the laundry and garage officers.

Best loved to pal around with politicos and civil servants when he visited the capitol in Denver. A publicity hound, he would invite droves of witnesses to view an execution and was personally involved in all phases of the proceedings. He carried out twenty-eight executions during his tenure and witnessed five others. He would personally escort the condemned man along the "last mile" to the gas chamber on the hill behind the prison.

But Best could be a softie too. When an eleven-year-old boy was sentenced for shooting his fifteen-year-old sister five times in the head with a rifle, Best took the boy into his own house instead of letting him go "inside the wall." He and his wife home-schooled the youngster for six months until Mrs. Best died. He then arranged for the boy to be sent to Father Flanagan's Boys' Town in Omaha rather than remanding him to the prison. The kindness never took, however, and the boy went on to lead a continued life of crime.

Best also installed an "electric eye" at the prison entrance to detect metal objects. This functioned like modern airport metal detectors and worked well, cutting down the contraband, especially guns, knives and ammunition.

His disciplinary practices proved less modern. His infamous "Old Gray Mare" was a beefed-up wooden sawhorse. Offending inmates would be strapped over it and flogged with brine-soaked leather straps. After the beating, the doctor examined the survivor to administer any necessary wound treatment. Roy commented after one episode of spanking, "Every once in a while I have to take this prison back from the convicts."

This kind of treatment finally caught up with Best. In 1951, after an attempted riot, five convicts were beaten on The Old Gray Mare. There was sufficient public uproar that Governor Thornton abolished physical punishment at all Colorado state institutions. Best was brought up on charges of violating the prisoner's civil rights and was suspended from his position. The suspension was especially awkward, as Roy was then serving his second term as president of the prestigious American Association of Wardens and Superintendents.

Best was unrepentant. "How can we handle these toughies? If my guards see one of those murderers going over the wall, what're they supposed to do, warn the prisoner he is going to lose his canteen privileges, or blow 'em to hell off the wall?" Two years later, acquitted of the charges and three days before taking the reins of the prison again, he had a heart attack and died.

TWENTY-SIX

A FAMILY OF PRISONS

When a convicted criminal is sentenced to prison, he's not plunked down in a random facility; he's sent to a specific type of prison. Colorado has five levels of prisons. In Cañon City we've got 'em all.

A Medium Security, Level III prison like Territorial is where most convicts start out. Dorm rooms. Communal bathrooms. Pretty much like what you see in the movies.

Level I and II, lower security facilities like forestry camps, might not even have a fence. Skyline and Four Mile fall into this category. Good behavior or lesser crimes can earn a place in these spots. Most prison escapes are from these facilities, with inmates just walking away from the prison or an outside work detail.

Level V facilities, like CSP, are for the more violent, predatory or insane inmates. With few exceptions, a felon has to earn his way into these. Most start out in a general population Level III prison where inmates mingle with one another, share cells, eat together in a chow hall, and take recreation together. However, this environment is a hunting ground for sexual predators, violent sociopaths, extortionists, gang kingpins, and wannabes. When these criminals ply their trades in a general population prison and get caught, the next and often final stop for them is CSP. Then they become my patients.

Level IV prisons, like Centennial next door to CSP, are sort of half-way houses between the extreme isolation of 23/7 lockdown in administrative segregation (ad seg) and the more social general population prisons. When San Carlos, the state facility for the criminally insane, is full up, a lot of the non-violent mentally ill inmates end up at Level IV. I got to take care of them too.

———

What's so special about CSP besides me being there? As a supermax prison it's the last stop on the penology scale. The philosophy behind these ultra-secure penitentiaries is to identify the most dangerous and disruptive criminals, remove them from general population prisons, and segregate these inmates so they can't harm others or themselves. It makes the general population prisons safer and easier to control. But you've got to put the bad boys somewhere, and that somewhere in Colorado is CSP.

The idea behind supermax prisons arose from a choice about how to handle prison troublemakers. The prison system could either break them up and isolate them from others of their kind, or concentrate them all in one big pot away from other inmates.

In 1933, J. Edgar Hoover opted for the latter solution by establishing a maximum-security facility at the former military prison on Alcatraz Island in San Francisco Bay. It lasted thirty years before closing due to the high cost of maintaining the deteriorating facility. A replacement ultra-secure federal prison opened in Marion, a sleepy town in southern Illinois nestled against the Shawnee National Forest.

The security turned out to be suboptimal. In 1975 one of the inmates, an electrician, was allowed to work on the electronic locks on all the doors in the main corridor. He converted a radio into a remote control unit, popped the locks and walked out the front door with four of his buddies.

Marion was also the site of one of the first helicopter escape attempts. In 1978 forty-three-year-old Barbara Oswald hijacked a St. Louis-based helicopter and forced the pilot to land in the prison yard at

Marion in an attempt to free her friend, inmate Garrett Trapnell. The escape was foiled when the pilot wrestled the gun from Oswald and shot her to death.

Not to be deterred, later that year Oswald's seventeen-year-old daughter, Robin, hijacked TWA Flight 541 from Louisville and forced the plane to land at Williamson County Regional Airport near Marion. She threatened to detonate dynamite strapped to her body if Trapnell was not released. FBI negotiators were able to talk her out of the plan, later discovering that the sticks of dynamite were really railroad flares attached to a doorbell.

In 1983 members of the Aryan Brotherhood gang killed two Marion prison guards in separate incidents. Lax security procedures allowed a prisoner, while walking down a hall, to turn to the side and approach a particular cell where a confederate unlocked his handcuffs with a stolen key and slipped him a knife.

As a result the prison went into permanent lockdown, thereby becoming the prototypical supermax prison. As Marion aged over the next thirty years, it was downgraded to a medium security facility, creating the need for a more modern federal supermax.

In 1994, the federal government opened an ultra-secure facility in Florence, Colorado just a few miles from today's CSP. I drove by Florence on the way to work every day.

Florence sounded a lot like my home at CSP, but a little more high-tech. Florence has cells with furniture of poured concrete including a bed, desk, and stool. The toilet shuts off if plugged and the shower runs on a timer to prevent flooding. Cell walls and plumbing are sound-proofed to prevent communication. An electric light, radio, and TV are all remotely controlled and out of direct contact with the inmate. These are treated as privileges that can be withdrawn for infractions. Inmates exercise in what has been described as an "empty swimming pool" so they don't know their location within the facility.

The windows also are oriented so the inmate doesn't know his location, as he can only see a patch of sky and roof through them. The names of the occupants read like yesterday's headlines with bombers, terrorists, spies, murderers, and gang kingpins on ice. All the guys you've seen on the national news are at Florence. A former Florence warden described the facility as "a cleaner version of Hell."

The question of supermax confinement comes down to two opposed views. One emphasizes the safety of the prison staff, other inmates, and the public who depend on us doing our job of keeping the bad guys locked up. The other view promotes the desire to rehabilitate and reintegrate prisoners back into society. It's tempting to throw away the key for a lot of these inmates, but remember that most of them will be released at some point.

I know as a staff member, I felt a lot safer in the supermax environment than when I worked in a general population prison. The supermax inmates may be "the worst of the worst," but at least they're behind bars.

———◆———

With one inmate per room, space in the supermax goes fast. Like dust and cellulite, crime never sleeps, so Colorado decided to build another supermax prison, tentatively named CSP II, to house the overflow.

CSP II is an appendage to Centennial, the old supermax across the road from CSP. I covered Centennial's clinic, so I watched each day as orange plastic barriers shifted, bulldozers dozed and convoys of cement trucks trundled in and out of the site.

When completed, CSP II will be the biggest and most modern supermax prison on earth. Its capacity of 1000 Level V inmates exceeds the 750 of CSP and is double the size of the federal government's supermax prison just down the road in Florence.

Attached by an underground umbilical, CSP II dwarfs Centennial. It's like a basketball tethered to a grape. Monolithic slabs of dull concrete with tiny slit windows rise five stories above Centennial's former parking lot. It's all panels, angles and corners like a deranged mass of grey Legos. No trim. No arches. No porticos. CSP II is just a big depressing lump. I think the same architect who designed the bunkers on the Maginot Line must have done this one.

I had a sneaking suspicion the CDOC budget wouldn't include another physician for CSP II, so I wrangled a spot on a tour of the partially completed behemoth to see where I might be practicing. Our group of ten gathered in the Centennial lobby, got outfitted with Day-Glo vests, safety glasses, and hard hats, and trooped into CSP II through a labyrinthine underground tunnel.

CSP II is huge. Beyond huge. Ginormous. Although being in any partially completed building is a little disorienting, my entire tour group was immediately and irrevocably lost. Even our guide kept sneaking looks at his map to figure out exactly where we were.

Pipes the size of tree trunks snaked overhead next to bazillions of data cables. Boilers like condominiums filled cavernous gray concrete rooms. Contract workers and low-security prisoners from Arrowhead and Four Mile prisons munched sandwiches on break and watched our entourage shuffle by like winos watching tourists in Times Square.

The State of Colorado must have gotten another deal from Home Depot, because *every single wall* was painted light beige. Miles and miles of beige. Acres of beige. Leagues of beige.

The overall effect was an acute sense of color deprivation. One of the elephantine compressors in the maintenance room had sucked out all the color in the universe, leaving an albino wilderness. The only color in the place, our little Day-Glo troupe floated along like flower petals on a snowfield.

"Here's medical," our guide announced in the middle of a featureless corridor. Of course. No windows. A new hyper-digital multi-million dollar prison of the future and still not one freaking window in the whole medical complex. Would it have killed them?

The cells themselves were state-of-the-art. They looked to be about seven-by-fifteen feet with a one-by-three-foot vertical window. At least the prisoners had a window, unlike the trolls in medical.

Color finally showed up in the paint scheme of the cell doors. "That's so they show up differently on the cameras," our guide said. "They've been doing tests and decided on alternating cell doors purple and yellow." Oh, gorp. The purple was a kind of faded grayish hue with the yellow coming in somewhere around vomit. The first executions in this place should be the decorators.

Each cell was a modular self-contained stainless steel shell made by inmates right there at Arrowhead and Four Mile, the minimum-restricted security prisons. While CSP II was being built they stockpiled the prefabricated cells into unused buildings around the East Cañon Complex like bales of hay. I don't know what the inmates thought of the whole process, but it wasn't the first time Colorado prisoners made their own jail. Territorial, the first Colorado State Penitentiary, was built almost entirely with inmate labor.

———

C DOC lost the physician at Fort Lyon Correctional Facility near Las Animas to retirement, so I was volunteered to go spend a couple of days there helping them catch up. That doesn't sound so bad, but FLCF is three hours away from home; an hour south to Pueblo then two hours straight out onto the eastern Colorado prairie.

It had been snowing for almost two days when my trusty CDOC pool car and I turned left at Pueblo and headed into the January wilderness. There's not much between Pueblo and Ft. Lyon. The two-lane blacktop had turned to a sheet of ice and the prairie winds screamed across the vacant landscape. The white edges of the road crept closer and closer to the center line, finally completely obscuring the asphalt. Where were all the cars? For that matter, where was the road?

I seem fated to blunder into dead-end road trips. Sky-Line Drive was bad enough, but now with the blowing snow piling up on my windward side, I realized I was at the mercy of the servicing skills of the inmate motor pool. I crept forward, the only car with a driver stupid enough to be crossing the plains in a blizzard. Four-wheel drive? Fuggetaboutit.

Let's see. Checklist. Blanket? Nope. Flashlight? Nada. Food? Water? A half-can of Diet Coke. This was the classic greenhorn-blunders-into-wilderness scenario. Was the engine running a little rough? Was that the baying of the wolf pack?

But no, it was the snowplow clearing the parking lot at the Mexican restaurant. Saved! Apparently the prairie folk were used to this kind of weather, because the place was packed. Best margaritas I've ever tasted. Fortified, I stumbled off to the Best Western.

Fort Lyon is CDOC's answer to the need for a nursing home. Originally an army post constructed in 1860, it was shamefully the base for the expedition that slaughtered a Cheyenne village in what came to be known as the Sand Creek Massacre.

The fort was residence to Kit Carson, who had come to be treated by the physician there. Not an auspicious choice as it turned out, as Carson died there of a ruptured aortic aneurism. After passing through iterations as a naval hospital, a tuberculosis sanitarium and a VA psychiatric hospital, CDOC finally picked it up.

The sun was already melting the snow as I drove past the entrance to the National Cemetery along the tree-lined avenue to the Fort Lyon parking lot. The salmon-brick buildings, some listed with the historic registry, formed a huge quadrangle with additional guest houses outside the prison walls.

Master control buzzed me through to the clinic proper. Assigned to a tiny office, it quickly became apparent why the facility was backed up.

Where my CSP inmates were usually fairly healthy and presented with perhaps one or two treatable disorders, Fort Lyon residents came in with five or six serious diseases layered one on top of another. Many were so infirm they couldn't escape if you gave them a bus ticket.

My habit before this was to listen to a patient, formulate a treatment plan and then document the whole encounter in the computer. That didn't work at Fort Lyon.

My tiny rowboat of memory capacity was inundated with a tsunami of complaints, diseases, medications and potential courses of action for each patient. I wrote out a separate sheet for each disease. Then I cross-referenced what I wanted to do for disease number one against what complications that would cause to diseases two through eight.

Arnold Dowgen, a fiftyish inmate who looked closer to eighty, had been in the CDOC system so long he'd forgotten why he was there. I met him my first day at Fort Lyon, struggling to get his wheelchair through the narrow clinic doorway.

I turned the first page of a voluminous chart. "Mr. Dowgen, it looks like you've been having some trouble with your diabetes."

"Better than it used to be, Doc. I ain't gone into a coma for over a year."

"Well, that's great, but your sugars are still running pretty high."

"Yeah, but the insulin screws up my potassium from the kidney disease."

Flipping more pages, I mutter, "Kidney disease... Oh, yeah. I see here they've had you on some lisinopril for..."

"Didn't work worth a damn. Thought I'd cough my head off. So they put me back on that other one for my blood pressure, but I peed my pants so bad I had to quit that too."

Falling rapidly behind the curve, I found the problem list that ran to forty items. "So this problem with the diabetes..."

"That's what put me in this thing," he said, pounding the armrest on the wheelchair.

Looking down the list, I started, "I thought that was because of the arthritis in your knees?"

"Nope. They ain't as bad as the shoulders anyway. Can't hardly push this thing around. No, it's the ulcers on my feet. I can't walk on 'em. Damn things won't heal."

Trying a new tack, I asked about his cholesterol medications.

"Never could get the right stuff, I guess. Muscle cramps with that first one they had me on. Last one turned me red as a beet. I give up on it."

We proceeded through the list, marking off past therapeutic failures and discussing the dwindling supply of new possibilities. Arnold was game to try about anything, but then again, he'd *already* tried about everything. This was going to be a long day.

I made one of my biggest mistakes at noon. The nurses offered to get me lunch from the kitchen. I didn't bring one, so I accepted. I felt like Bear Grylls in one of his look-at-me-eat-this sessions. Never again.

The saving graces for Fort Lyon were the evening margaritas and the change of pace from the constant bitching of CSP prisoners. The Fort Lyon guys had real diseases instead of the fantasies so popular back at the East Cañon Complex. Maybe because they realized they really needed help, they were generally more mature and easier to work with. I didn't have to throw a single person out of the clinic.

———

San Carlos Correctional Facility; the CDOC prison for the criminally insane, is located on the grounds of the Colorado Mental Health Institute in Pueblo (CMHIP). I never got the chance to see patients there, but we had provider meetings there a few times. One of my neighbors, a hard-rock miner turned psychologist, worked there for a time. He provided me with enough stories to make me glad I was safe at CSP.

CMHIP has the cachet of an aging industrial park. Ancient rusting buildings huddled beside a potholed serpentine asphalt drive. Skeletal communication aerials from the fifties drooped from tarred roofs. Dented fifty-five gallon drums pushed against the buildings lacked only a clutch of winos to complete the picture. San Carlos was relegated to the back of CMHIP with a wide parking lot and the novelty of an entrance without razor wire.

The cramped lobby carried forward the depressed theme with a diminutive balcony peeking over the control station and cramped corridors leading off to unmarked destinations. Our meetings were on the second floor. This entailed crowding into a tiny elevator in a prison mental hospital; the stuff of B-movies.

All I can say about the rest of the facility was that I declined the tour. I don't know what it was about the place, but I felt better in the bowels of the supermax than I did at San Carlos.

CSP tends to be the dumping ground for San Carlos overflow. When an inmate is mentally ill and is violent or otherwise disruptive, they go to San Carlos. Unless they're full up. Then they're sent to the only place they can be segregated from other prisoners and closely monitored: CSP.

When the staff at CSP can't stand the antics of a particular mentally ill offender anymore, we ship him to San Carlos. San Carlos retaliates by sending us someone even worse. These cases get bounced back and forth regularly, but at least it gives the staff a rest from a specific inmate's brand of craziness.

The problem with mentally ill inmates isn't just that they disrupt others. It goes both ways. Inmates are quick to take advantage of the mentally ill with sexual predation, intimidation, and extortion. Thus, the isolation of CSP protects the mentally ill inmates from predators.

The only problem I had working with the mentally ill patients was that they were crazy. Besides the increased likelihood of an unprovoked attack, I found it hard to put together a medical program with someone who wasn't rational. These were the guys who complained we were shooting poison gas or mind-control agents into their air vents.

When someone gives you a pill, there has to be a certain amount of trust involved in taking it. Frequently with the mentally ill population, it just wasn't there. August Courtman, a former plumber and habitual thief, transferred to CSP from the San Carlos pool.

"Mr. Courtman, the nurses tell me you're not taking your thyroid medicine."

"Damn straight. I know what you're trying to pull."

"What exactly would that be?"

"I seen those blue pills. Turns you into a zombie. No fuckin' way you get me to take that."

"Has anyone ever talked to you about your thyroid?"

"Bullshit. Nothin' wrong with me. You just try to make me take that, and we'll see what happens."

"This isn't one of your mental health meds. It's for your thyroid. You know how cold you get? This'll help that."

"Punch your fuckin' lights out you come near me with that shit."

This was a losing battle. Since not taking his thyroid medication wouldn't actually kill him, I had to let it go.

There's a large group of chronically depressed inmates as well. They were more frustrating for me to deal with because I never knew if I was getting through at all. Leroy Tipton, a child molester from Limon, was on some fairly heavy-duty antidepressants courtesy of my mental health colleagues, but I couldn't tell as he sat on the gurney for a chronic care visit, shoulders hunched, staring at the floor.

"Mr. Tipton, I see you've had trouble with high cholesterol before."

Leroy might have screwed up his mouth a little, but otherwise remained mute.

"I see in your record that you used to take some medicine for that. Was that something you wanted to get started again?"

Leroy shrugged.

I pointed to my chest. "Mr. Tipton, I'm over here."

Leroy didn't actually move his head, but rolled his eyes in my general direction, then back to neutral.

I tried the proactive approach. "Your cholesterol was pretty high on your last lab. How about if I start you back on the medication to bring it down?"

Another shrug.

"Would that be okay with you? Would you take it?"

Nothing. I could have been talking to a lump of oatmeal.

"Mr. Tipton, I need some kind of answer. The medicine. Yes or no?"

A barely perceptible head movement. "Don't care."

"I'll take that as a yes, you'll try it."

"Whatever."

Sometimes patients like Leroy will shape up as their antidepressants kick in. Often it ends with the nurses reporting that Leroy won't get out of bed to get the pill at medline. Other than wishing my mental health buddies good luck, I have to chalk up another one in the loss column.

If Colorado has a country club prison, it's Four Mile. While it lacks a golf course and tennis courts, it sports a baseball diamond, a soccer field, two running tracks, five handball courts, two huge weightlifting areas with rubber flooring, six basketball courts, a half dozen horseshoe pits, two shuffleboard courts and a full-size beach volleyball court complete with sand, referee's box, and bleachers. Picnic tables festoon the areas between activities. I'm not sure they're going to have room for the Ferris wheel. But wait. There's more.

A separate fenced area tucked behind one of the residence halls is home to the Indian sweat lodge complete with stacks of firewood and a framework for the fabric tent. As Dave Barry might say, I am not making this up.

I got a call from my HSA. He wanted to know if I would transfer from CSP and Centennial to cover Four Mile and Arrowhead prisons. Still part of the East Cañon Complex, these prisons were general population, lower security facilities. I'd been there a few times for meetings. I knew they had clinics above ground with actual windows. This good fortune made me suspicious.

It turned out that the doctor at Four Mile wanted to transfer to CSP because he thought the workload would be lighter at the supermax. *Is he in for a surprise*, I thought.

I learned he was working nights and weekends to keep up with his charting. No extra pay. "How dedicated," said the HSA. *What a moron,* I thought.

I'd been at CSP and Centennial for over three years at that point. I struggled with my relations with the CSP administrator who still wanted to play doctor and micromanage everything. Maybe time for a change. I went for it.

A Level II, minimum-restrictive facility, Four Mile has a single perimeter fence topped with desultory flops of razor wire appearing almost as an afterthought compared to the aggressive tangles of wire jammed into every corner of Centennial, Fremont and CSP. It doesn't matter; nobody wants to leave.

The herd of 800 cattle next door is a notorious feature of Four Mile. Depending on which way the wind is blowing, the interior of the prison can get pretty ripe.

Where there are cows, there are birds. Lots of birds. Before the budget cuts, the administration offered free weekly car washes to the Four Mile staff. Now they've installed electronic recordings of some bird of prey in the parking lot. I'm not sure what it's supposed to be, probably a hawk or maybe a raptor. In any case, I can't see that the birds pay any attention to the faux squawks. At the other prisons, staffers walk to their cars chatting amiably. At Four Mile, they're looking up. I was reminded of my true status at Four Mile when I left for the day and heard the raptor scream above the white blotches on my car.

The medical unit was a real clinic with (gasp!) a window. A big one. This was such a psychological boost after being buried in the concrete of CSP and Centennial that I had trouble adjusting at first. I mean, it was like...sunshine!

My office was well stocked and actually kind of comfy, except for the ice machine. For reasons known only to administrators, they decided that putting a commercial ice machine in the physician's office would be a good idea. It wasn't.

Between gurgling plumbing, the crash of tumbling ice cubes, and the roar of the compressor, I couldn't hear myself think. The first day at Four Mile I disabled the beast. No ice, but now I had a shot at hearing a heart murmur.

My Four Mile patients were a happy group. They knew they had it good, and were not about to screw it up. They even held the door for me and practically bowed as I walked past. I saw Evan Koski, a petty thief from Eagle, during my first week.

"So how's the cholesterol medicine going, Mr. Koski?"

"Great, Doc. How do the numbers look?"

Turning the chart around, I went through the different lab results, all pretty good.

"Look at that cholesterol, Doc. It never was that good on the outside."

"The triglycerides are better too, but we could tune that up a little bit."

"Whatever you say, Doc. You know how to handle it best."

Whenever an inmate started giving me compliments, it means either he's lying or he wants something he shouldn't have. In the case of the Four Mile inmates, though, there was less flattery and more genuine appreciation. Quite a change from the hostility of CSP. I thought of the doctor I'd switched with to get here and chuckled. Poor bastard.

Everything was wonderful. Except. Herman, my old HSA, followed me. Not in flesh, but in spirit. I now had a brand-new HSA, Todd, with a background as a chiropractor. Before I met him, I hoped that the idea to actually accomplish something with your time might be a shared trait. Not.

First it was the lunch thing again. *You Don't Get a Lunch* should be embossed on every CDOC employee's ID card. Even though the clinic is shut down for two hours from eleven to one, I was informed that setting foot outside was forbidden. If I brought in a brown bag, then Todd might look the other way, but taking a break to go outside in the fresh air would result in docked pay.

Like my old nemesis, Todd was clear about his expectations. After not having lunch, the next priority was to be physically present and to write voluminous chart notes.

My physician predecessor at Arrowhead and Four Mile was thorough. Really, really thorough. He would make a tortoise go mad with impatience. He was famous for chart reviews, sitting for hours simply reviewing all the old information in a medical chart. He wouldn't see the actual patient, mind you, he just reviewed the endless, mind-numbingly irrelevant data in the dusty records. He apparently loved it.

If he happened to see a patient, he would employ the same agonizingly glacial pace in interviewing and recording every syllable that wandered randomly from the inmate's mouth. His notes were masterpieces of bloat and irrelevancy. If a doctor in the real world employed this method, he could write a biography four generations deep from his clinical notes, but he'd be broke in a week.

I'm a cut-to-the-chase kind of guy. If I'm seeing an inmate for high blood pressure, I don't want to talk about his backache or the fact that his grandmother died of the plague.

Todd, my new HSA, disagreed. He gave me one of my colleague's chart notes as a paragon to emulate. It ran to three single-spaced typed pages. Todd loved puffery. Lots of words on a page indicated quality medicine, which, in turn, translated to good reviews for him.

The final blow to my nascent relationship with Todd came after about a week. He entered my office looking administratively regretful.

"Dr. Wright, I noticed a book on your desk."

"Yes. I always bring a book to work. Want to borrow it?"

"I'm going to pretend I didn't see it."

"Okay. Pretend away. Is there some problem with books?"

"I can always give you more patients."

"Actually, I don't think you can. I'm already seeing four times as many patients as the last person to occupy this chair, and I get finished on time."

Todd, struggling for a comeback, tapped my book disapprovingly and displayed a concerned frown. It seemed this required some explanation.

"I read the book while I'm not going outside for the lunch I don't get."

"I'm trying to cut you some slack. Don't let it happen again."

"Are you referring to the book or letting you into my office?"

Apparently feeling he had made his point, Todd harrumphed away.

One of the first things I learned at CDOC was to never enter any prison without a book. Inmates create gaps in the schedule by refusing to come for appointments; facilities regularly lock down for real and simulated emergencies; count time can be endless; employees occasionally sneak lunch. During these periods the options are to either stare blankly at the wall, gossip with the nurses, or read a book. Todd was apparently of the blank wall school. I considered surfing for porn sites, but all the good ones were blocked.

TWENTY-SEVEN

CMRC

I worked three long days a week in Cañon City so I wouldn't have to commute so often. This left me with four days a week of leisure. At first it was great. I love to hike in the mountains, but on howling cold Colorado days when I sat propped on the couch I grew restless. About this time May, one of the physician assistants at Centennial, asked me if I would be interested in an extra day job.

She worked at Cheyenne Mountain Re-entry Center (CMRC) as a second job. Apparently, everyone there hated the facility doctor. "She's a total drama queen," May said. "'Do this. Get that. I don't do that.' She's a gigantic pain. It's only one day a week. Would you be interested?"

"So what kind of place is this?" I asked.

"A re-entry center. These are guys with a short time on their sentence. They're ready for discharge, parole, halfway house, that kind of stuff. Same kind of thing you're doing here, but nicer clientele. And it's in the Springs, so you don't have a monster commute. Piece of cake."

"I don't know if—"

"And they pay better than CDOC."

"Sounds good. I'm in."

CMRC, a prison owned and operated by a private corporation, has a deal with CDOC to take care of lower security prisoners without serious health problems. They didn't have the facilities to care for them, and sick prisoners cost too much anyway. This was a bottom-line kind of place.

CMRC's home on Las Vegas Avenue in Colorado Springs has little in common with its more illustrious namesake to the southwest. No limos, no casinos, not even a neon light. A gravel pit, the police impound lot, and a salvage yard pretty much set the tone for the neighborhood. It fit, depressingly, the location of a bottom-line kind of prison.

The facility occupies a nondescript monolithic three-story salmon brick building fighting for space among clouds of tumbleweeds and anemic cottonwoods along the shallow banks of Fountain Creek, the town's only claim to a river. Aside from the lack of windows, it could have been an office building in any B-grade industrial park.

I parked next to a concrete pit ringed with chain link and razor wire. Peering over the edge I could see six half-court basketball goals and a couple of weight benches. Not much as far as recreational facilities go, but a lot better than a solitary room with a chin-up bar at CSP.

I trudged up a set of steep concrete stairs to the entry vestibule. Next to the stairway was the world's longest wheelchair ramp, plunging down the side of the building like a roller-coaster to a hairpin turn into the parking lot. Any wheelchair losing its brakes on that thing would end up in Kansas.

The outer door of the vestibule was unlocked, but the gray inner door wasn't. There was a button. To push or to wait? I didn't want to piss anyone off before I was even in the building. I waited. Nothing.

Another staff member came in, reached across and pushed the button, giving me a querulous look. "New kid," I said and he nodded.

We were buzzed into the CMRC version of a sally port. I put my tote bag on the pass-through and gave the grim-faced woman a medium-wattage smile.

"You are...?" she said.

"Dr. Wright." I held out my CDOC badge. "I'm the new medical doctor."

I didn't expect her to click her heels and salute, but I hoped for at least a little sign of acknowledgement. I didn't get it.

"What's that?" she said, pointing to my black canvas tote bag.

"Lunch," I said. "And my stethoscope."

"You can't bring that in here," she said flatly.

"What? You don't eat lunch either?"

"The bag. You can't bring a black bag in here. Has to be transparent."

"I don't have a transparent tote bag. Look, it's open at the top," I said, spreading it open.

"Don't touch the bag," she said.

This was not going well. "I just brought it in. I'm not going to steal it."

She peered into the bag and brought out a liter of tea. "Can't bring this in," she said.

"Tea is contraband?"

"Can't bring in over sixteen ounces of liquid."

This felt a lot like airport security. "Should I take off my shoes too?" I asked facetiously.

"Yep. Belt too."

She continued her search, pulling out my PDA. "Can't bring this in."

"It's CDOC issue. Look at the stamp on the back."

She looked and muttered something. Next she found my stethoscope. "Never seen one like this. Can't bring it in."

"It's electronic. Like an amplifier. Not explosive."

"I'll have to get clearance on this."

"Fine. Call the HSA in medical. She'll vouch for me."

I couldn't help wondering why the same bag I took breezily into the state's only supermax prison was now being dissected piece by piece to get into a minimum restrictive re-entry center. Calls were made. Approvals given. I made it through the metal detector.

The staff officer buzzed the exit door and looked at me with a, "Well, what are you waiting for?" expression.

"Where's medical?" I asked.

Now absolutely positive she had an idiot on her hands, she picked up the phone and called one of the nurses to come and give me an escort.

Paloma, a perky nurse from the Dominican Republic, soon arrived and led me through halls with giant lettered posters proclaiming,

"Anger Is One Letter Away From Danger," "Make Better Choices," and "Get Out – Stay Out."

We proceeded through electronic doors to a huge stairwell. "Let me guess," I said. "Medical is in the basement. No windows." She smiled and held the door. "After you."

Inmates, dressed in dark green scrubs, marched up and down like Oompa Loompas. For reasons unclear, the stairs to the basement covered not one story, but a vertiginous two. The same guy who designed the wheelchair ramp outside must have put in the stairs.

Stenciled in script above the stairwell door was the single word, *Aspen.* I raised an eyebrow. "Aspen?"

"Breckenridge is the next floor up," Paloma said.

"Little joke?" I said.

Paloma nodded. "Little."

I craned up at the endless steps ascending into misty nether. "Must be popular with the troops," I said. "How many floors?"

"Two more levels above this one," Paloma said. "Our most frequent request is to get an elevator pass."

Paloma and I huffed down to medical. Sally, my Health Services Administrator, had the look of someone fighting a forest fire with a squirt gun. "Glad you're here. This is your office. Ask the nurses for anything you need. Gotta go."

My office, subterranean as always, had sheetrock walls. More cheerful than concrete block but still painted beige. A cabinet inspection revealed a better assortment of supplies than CDOC provided. It was like a real clinic with Band-Aids and everything.

May, my PA from CDOC, came in to show me the computer system. "It's the same system CDOC uses, but it connects remotely," she said.

"No problem. I'm used to that."

"It's slow," she said.

"CDOC's system has always been slow."

"No, I mean it's *really* slow," May said.

"How could it be slower? It would have to run in reverse."

"They had an administrator in charge of setting up the system. The company gave him a pile of cash and said he could keep the change after he set it up."

"So he picked the cheapest system he could find," I said.

"Beyond cheap. Dial up."

"Dial up? Nobody's used dial up for thirty years. The system wouldn't even be functional."

"Apparently he found somebody with spare parts who put the system together with duct tape. I think they're both on the beach in Acapulco."

Turns out she was right. With dropped connections and lag time they wouldn't put up with in Siberia, the computer system made CDOC's look like a gazelle. I had time to read all the little message boxes that usually flash by when you boot up. The one that stayed up the longest informed me that FART.EXE was initializing. I should have known.

I'm a pretty good typist. I typed a paragraph while looking at the patient's chart then glanced up at the computer screen. Blank. The cursor wasn't moving. The mouse was inactive. Every indication of digital death. Then v-e-r-y s-l-o-w-l-y, letter by painful letter, the text crawled, gasping across the screen like arthritic ants. It took longer for the text to appear than it did for me to type it.

"You're kidding," I said.

May shrugged.

"Where's the pharmacy?"

"Not there. They use a separate one. It's on a website."

"But we have a medical record system, such as it is, right here."

She smiled the patient smile of a mother with a slow child then logged onto the pharmacy website and entered the prescription. Instead of an entry appearing on the screen, a little whirring sound started on top of a filing cabinet. A short row of stick-on labels crawled from a mini-printer.

"You're kidding," I said. It seemed to be the phrase of the day.

"Nope," she said, peeling a label and sticking it on the patient encounter sheet. "And don't forget to stick another one in the back of the chart where all the medicines are listed."

"Doesn't this kind of defeat the purpose of an electronic medical record?" I asked. "I mean, you can't transmit sticky labels from place to place. You can't look them up in a database, even if the little laser printer is kind of cute."

"It's not a laser printer. It's carbon paper."

"Carbon paper? A computer that prints with carbon paper? Can it print with White-Out if I make a mistake?"

This is the twenty-first century. Why would someone buy a printer that uses carbon paper? Ah! Someone with a warehouse of antique printers and a buddy in procurement who was having a good time in Acapulco.

The work was pretty much like what I'd been doing at CDOC, but the setup was more like a regular medical clinic with a waiting room and attached nursing station. A key card unlocked a door to the hallway leading to my office.

I realized right away this would never fly at CSP. There were no COs that came back with the inmates to my office. I was behind an electronically locked door in a remote office. In an emergency, nobody up front could even hear me let alone come to my aid. But was I worried? Well, yes.

At least I had some experience dealing with inmates. I thought I had a pretty good handle on when things were likely to turn ugly. Usually about the time I said, "No."

To help people get where they were needed, CMRC had a PA system. No email or personal radios for these guys. Just shout it out. Unlike CSP, they invested in quality speakers. Big ones. Having the speaker right outside the exam room made it easy to appreciate the quality of the sound. The reflective qualities of the bare walls seemed to focus the sound right about at my desk chair.

Tommie Felipe was a young Hispanic mechanic with a sideline career in an automobile chop shop. He'd done a year in CDOC and was now on the launching pad at CMRC with four months to go before hitting the streets again. I called him down to the clinic to discuss his cholesterol lab results.

"Mr. Felipe, let me explain these lab results. You see—" ATTENTION IN THE FACILITY!! ATTENTION IN THE FACILITY!! SCOTT 135679, ANDERSON 119754, MURPHY 99237, JONES 103227 REPORT TO INTAKE IMMEDIATELY!! I REPEAT. SCOTT 135679, ANDERSON 119754, MURPHY 99237, JONES 103227 REPORT TO INTAKE IMMEDIATELY!!

"Sorry about that. Now here is—" ATTENTION IN THE FACILITY!! ATTENTION IN THE FACILITY!! SERGEANT ADAMS REPORT TO LAUNDRY!! REPEAT. SERGEANT ADAMS REPORT TO LAUNDRY!!

"Let's start over. When I got this blood test, I was looking for—" ATTENTION IN THE FACILITY!! ATTENTION IN THE FACILITY!! RECREATION TIME IS NOW ENDED!! REPEAT. RECREATION TIME IS NOW ENDED!!

"Mr. Felipe, I'll send you a memo about the test results."

This went on endlessly all day. There were announcements for inmate movement, count time, end of count, start and end of recreation, birthdays, Uruguayan national holidays, breaking news in the Balkans, acquisition of more powerful amplifiers for the PA system, and other critical topics too numerous to mention. If I wasn't deaf before...

The CMRC inmates had a different attitude from those at CSP. For one thing, the CMRC people were guilty. They even told me so. They talked about how they screwed up and that they are never coming back to prison. There were lots of comments about their plans once they got out in a month or two. Many had family, a place to live, and even a job lined up. All this was in stark contrast to the CSP crowd.

At CSP nobody was guilty. They just got caught. Guilt had nothing to do with it, since they saw nothing wrong with what they did in the first place. Hell, they'd do it again if given the chance, and they often did.

Unlike the CMRC inmates, rarely did anyone at CSP talk about plans for the future. Vinnie Ambrose, a CSP inmate just finishing a ten-year sentence for extortion, was typical when I asked him about his goals after release: "I dunno. Guess I'll go to Texas." Great plan. At least if he made it to the Colorado line, I wouldn't have to see him again.

Many CSP inmates expected to be back in prison or dead within a few months of release, and they often made good on that ambition. I thought inmates would be more interested in chronic care issues as a release date approached, but often it was the opposite. Matt Warren, a bigwig with the Aryan Brotherhood, gave me his take during a clinic visit for his hypertension: "Shit, Doc, I ain't worried about blood pressure. I'll be dead in a month."

That's not to say that CMRC was a daycare center. It was still a grim place, but at least a tunnel with a light at the end. And they had motivational posters. All CSP had on the walls was a picture of a man holding his head with the caption "Rape is Wrong," or a poster on hepatitis C. Not nearly as motivating.

Although CMRC represented a better class of criminal, they still could be a pain in the ass. In general, the CSP inmates were more aggressive and demanding during their appointments, while the CMRC inmates were more whiney and needy. If CSP had the tantrum-throwing two year olds, CMRC had the angst-ridden teens.

Regardless of the kinder-gentler image, CMRC had its share of bad boys. These ended up in the Special Housing Unit or SHU, an area behind an unmarked steel door down the hall from medical. As the custodian of all things healthful, I was tasked to inspect the SHU once a week to make sure the cooties weren't taking over. It seemed kind of silly to walk around the two tiers of cells looking for dirty towels and dead rats. I told my wife, Mollie, that I inspected the SHU for cleanliness, and she fell over laughing. I'm not the world's neatest person.

TWENTY-EIGHT

CENTENNIAL SOUTH

I t's official. Apparently due to my exceptional clinical acumen, efficiency, and good looks, I was appointed to take care of all the inmates at Centennial South, the official name for CSP II, the new supermax. This was in addition to my regular duties at the old Centennial and CSP. I suppose I should have been flattered, but somehow I suspected not paying for another doctor was also part of the equation.

Even though construction continued, CDOC was already transferring inmates, so I went over to check it out.

The tunnel that connects the present Centennial prison with Centennial South is a long, snaking, airless passage with four sets of doors to pass through before you see the florescent light of day inside the new facility.

The first lesson in making the transit is: "Take a guy with a radio." There aren't any call buttons in the passage and there are lots of blind areas. Like where the doors are. So if you don't have a CO with a radio accompanying you to call master control and have them open the doors, you're likely to get stuck between doors in the tunnel for a *long* time. To paraphrase the old sci-fi movie, *Alien*, in the tunnel, nobody can hear you scream.

The tunnel houses a historical landmark in the old Centennial side of the prison. We passed a bricked-up entrance to a loading dock where

Terry Akers and six other inmates shot it out with prison guards in 1990 and briefly escaped. Akers smuggled in a couple of guns hidden inside cans of ink from the nearby printing shop.

Akers' plan was to release about twenty other prisoners, but after shooting and killing an officer in the gym where the first seven inmates were located, he found the officer's keys wouldn't open the cellblock to get the rest. He shot another officer before making his escape through the loading dock. Five of his fellow escapees were caught in the parking lot trying to steal a car, but Akers and another man headed south across the Arkansas River.

His companion was quickly rounded up, but Akers evaded capture until the next day when his boot prints led the escape team to a trailer near Florence. Although I'm sure it didn't happen, I heard rumors that his reward for shooting two officers was to get the living crap beaten out of him. Akers eventually became a resident at CSP and died of liver failure from chronic hepatitis C.

I learned some new protocols. Unlike CSP, you're supposed to press the call button when you come to a door. They've got so many cameras that there aren't enough monitors to show all the feeds. But if you push the call button, the camera corresponding to that button pops up front and center on the monitor bank. Cool. You might still wait forever, but at least they can see you.

The stairs are another story. With no keys and no camera coverage, it's easy to get locked in a stairwell. The same with the holding cells in the medical corridor. Unlike CSP, these cells aren't controlled electronically. They just close like a normal door.

A week before our tour, a sergeant was inspecting a holding cell for items left over by the construction crew when she heard a click behind her. Oops. She called on her radio for someone to "come over and help me out with something in medical." Nobody came. After several similar calls, she finally had to say that she'd locked herself in a holding cell and would somebody please come let her out? They came to her aid, but the entire radio network would never let her forget it.

Someone noticed that the huge lead-lined doors on the x-ray suite were installed backwards. They open in instead of out so you can open the doors, but you can't get into the room to do anything once they're open. And they're set in concrete. Oops.

We noticed bunches of minor slipups like putting down acres of sod outside only to discover that nobody thought to install a sprinkler system. We're in the desert here. Now we've got ten miles of garden hose supplying scores of portable sprinklers.

———

As soon as the beige paint was dry, CDOC started moving prisoners to Centennial South from the Limon and Crowley prisons, about fifteen to twenty coming each day. They seemed to be mostly inmates with "behavior problems." This meant violent and crazy.

The current prison administration is a big fan of mental health. My understanding was that they planned to hire twenty more mental health personnel for the new facility. Too bad they couldn't spring for another physician for the extra thousand inmates.

We were supposed to be getting "behavior problems" that were at least reasonably intelligent and healthy. I don't know about the behavior part yet, but I found myself checking in lots of people with some flavor of "stupid" as part of their diagnosis list. Not my bailiwick, however.

The healthy part seemed to have gone by the boards too. My average inmate at CSP had a "problem list" of their most significant diagnoses about half a page long. Some of the new guys had a couple of pages with a list of medications that would back up the line at Walgreen's for the better part of the day. I had a sneaking suspicion that we were getting dumped on with the most obnoxious, whining, and troublesome inmates from the other facilities. But it was just a suspicion. I mean, why would they do that?

———

One day I trudged up to the clinic at Centennial to find—nobody. The clinic was dark and empty, and I was freezing my butt outside the locked entry door. It felt like I'd come home and found my parents had moved out while I was in school. Must be in Centennial South next door.

I retraced my steps out of Centennial, around the grey concrete monolith of the new prison to the entrance of Centennial South. At least the lights were on.

I exchanged my chit for a ring of "Restricted Physician's Keys," which consisted of a single pathetic-looking key. I commandeered an escort to show me where the medical clinic was located. Thankfully, I didn't have to enter through the umbilical Tunnel O' Doom from the old Centennial. Still, it was a hike down a hundred-yard barren corridor to another control center and finally into the medical wing.

I felt like dropping breadcrumbs along the way, scanning any identifying door labels I could find to help me retrace my steps. One label proclaimed "Non-Lethal." Well, that was encouraging. But what about the next door? Nope, it said "Mental Health," which might have been a euphemism for the "Lethal" label. Just kidding.

While the sliding steel doors at CSP rattle, clank, and sputter like a rusting hawser chain, the ones at Centennial South first gave a hiss of compressed air, paused, and then glided open soundlessly as if on rubber tires. Elegant—and a little spooky.

Once in the clinical services section I still had to find my office. I saw familiar faces in the nursing station, but they were locked behind the steel and glass wall. I knocked and waved hopefully.

It turns out that *all* the doors were locked. Everywhere. Nurses in the nursing station were locked out of the adjacent medication room. The nursing station was locked from the medical corridor. All the examination rooms were locked. The offices, the break room, the copy room were all locked. Including my office.

Hooray! My one magic key opened all of them. I asked the nurses if it wasn't a gigantic pain to constantly be unlocking doors just to get about their business. Eyes rolled.

The nurses purchased a dozen doorstops to hold open the most frequently used doors. Then the fire marshal showed up and confiscated them all with the strict admonition that all doors were to remain closed and locked at all times.

This seemed a little harsh to me since cinderblock and concrete seldom burst into flame unprovoked, but who am I to question authority? It took me about an hour to round up a doorstop for my office. The newest contraband in the supermax.

The rest of the doors sprouted cardboard shims in their catches. Clever. The doors are closed (almost) but prevented from locking. If the marshal shows up again, we'll have enough warning to quickly pull them all out and innocently await his arrival. Personally, if the concrete walls are ever enveloped with flame, I'd rather get the hell out than fumble my way through keyed doors. Just saying.

I wandered down the echoing corridor to my new office, popped a CD into my computer and sat back as humanity exploded from the tiny speakers. I felt at home. Except for the bare concrete walls, steel doors, and bloodthirsty criminals. Just Handel and me.

———◆———

With a hundred prisoners transferred to Centennial South every week and a hundred new ones arriving at the old Centennial to take their places, the medical service was totally swamped. Besides the routine evaluations, we were inundated with kites from the new guys trying to get drugs or surgery that was denied at their old facility. On the second day of chaos in the clinic, Everett Bollig, a transfer from Limon serving twenty-five for auto theft, thought he'd try his luck.

"What seems to be the problem, Mr. Bollig?"

"I gotta get something for these seizures, Doc."

"You've got seizures?"

"All the time. Couple a week. Been going on for years."

I searched the chart from Limon. "There's no mention of any seizures at Limon."

"I had 'em all the time, but they wouldn't do nothin' about it."

"So you had seizures a couple of times a week at Limon, but nobody noticed?"

"Oh, they knew all about it, just wouldn't give me nothin'."

"And I'll bet you have something in mind."

"Neurontin, Doc. I took it all the time on the streets. The only thing that worked."

"Didn't your cellie notice you thrashing around on the floor?"

"Sure. We told the COs, but they never did nothin'."

"And nobody else saw these?"

"They happen at night."

"So it's real dark and nobody can see it."

"Right. Can you get me on those Neurontins again? They really helped."

"No. Notify the pod staff if you have a seizure and we'll get right on it."

Clearly the whole exchange was bullshit. Bollig never had seizures. He wanted the Neurontin to sell to other prisoners or maybe just for his own recreational use. Bollig knew we were swamped, and it would be lots easier just to grant every request and get on down the line.

The same went for inmates who had been denied their favorite medication, or who wanted their dosages or timing changed, or who had been denied an elective surgery. They figured I didn't know their history, so they gave it another shot.

I didn't mind the strategic omissions and general obfuscation the inmates tried to pull during a clinic visit. I expected that. What I found I couldn't stand was being lied to.

I understand that integrity is not the strong suit for my patients, but outright lies just frost me. I didn't understand this for a long time but finally decided that it meant the inmate thought I was stupid. So I wasn't just being misled. I was being insulted. If I caught an inmate in an outright lie, it was curtains for him. I remember one of my first visits with Aaron Brackett, a black fireplug of a man with ten more years to go on an assault charge. Transferred from Sterling to Centennial South, Aaron clogged up my clinic with a boatload of bogus complaints.

"Hello again, Mr. Brackett. What's the problem du jour?"

"I don't have no problem with that, Doc. It's my legs. Shooting pains down both sides. They said it was some kind of nerve damage at Sterling."

"I'll bet they gave you something for it too."

"Sure did, Doc. They said Percocet would be the best thing for it, but I got to be honest (uh-oh!), they finally just gave me that gabapentin stuff. It's not the best, but it really helps."

Several things are happening now. First, Aaron said he had to be honest. That means he's lying. Second, he said the medicos at Sterling thought Percocet would be the drug of choice. It isn't, and they don't ever use it at Sterling anyway. Third, he knew the generic name for Neurontin. That meant he'd done his homework about that particular drug and decided to target it. Inmates seldom know the names of the drugs prescribed to them, let alone the more complicated chemical or generic names. Hell, I can't even remember them. Fourth, my exam showed nothing wrong, let alone something that required Neurontin. I went for the clincher.

"Gabapentin, eh? What dose did they have you on?"

"Uh, 3600 a day, Doc."

Bingo. Even if they somehow know the name of the drug they're on, inmates never get the dose right. The fact that Aaron picked out the maximum allowable dose of gabapentin is another nail in the coffin.

A couple of minutes sufficed for this exchange. I pulled out his chart. "Wow, that's a big dose. Let's see what the guys at Sterling were thinking about this."

Seeing opportunity slipping away in the form of his written records, Aaron scrambled. "Maybe it wasn't that much. I think they cut it down to 1800."

Flipping through the chart, I feign a puzzled expression. "Gee, Mr. Brackett, I don't see any mention here of gabapentin at all. No leg pains either."

"But, I—"

"You were never on gabapentin, Mr. Brackett, for leg pains or anything else. You must have yourself confused with someone else. Looks like we're done here."

"No, I—"

"Done."

It's not that Brackett's story was so hard to handle; it was the fact that there were thirty or forty Bracketts arriving each day, and I didn't have time to sort the fantasy out from legitimate problems. I also had to see my regular clinic patients, even when I didn't eat the lunch I wasn't supposed to have.

It didn't help to have a social worker as HSA running the show. In medicine, when a bunch of catastrophes hit the ER at once, you triage. You see the sickest people first and the rest have to wait. In social work apparently there is no triage. Everyone gets seen right away.

Besides seeing all the regular clinic appointments, I had guys with chronic backaches queued up with diabetics slipping into coma. At this point I was rethinking my idea that this was the easiest job I ever had. The job itself still qualified as easy. It was only hard if you wanted to do it well and actually accomplish something useful.

A lthough all my patients were brought to the medical clinic, I wanted to see some more of the prison, so I trekked to L-pod to check out where the new inmates are housed.

The pod was a lot cleaner than my last visit. One little housekeeping item that slipped by were several hacksaw blades embedded in the surface of the concrete floors. They'd apparently found three so far. The story goes that inmates from Four Mile, the low security prison next door to Centennial South, were doing the concrete work and they kind of accidentally left some hacksaw blades in areas where they could be chipped free later. It sounds goofy enough to be true.

The doors in the cells were all color-coded in sequence: brown, yellow, purple, green, an expansion from the previous duotone scheme I'd seen previously. If a CO sees something out on the unit he can recognize which door is involved by the color instead of looking for numbers. Ugly as hell, but potentially a useful feature.

L-Pod has sections of three tiers with eight cells in each tier. They all face out toward a concrete wall instead of toward other cells so there's no visual contact among the cells at all. A Lexan-doored shower is on the far end of each unit facing the control center. Not a lot of privacy, but that's the point.

I went up into the pod control center; a video-game freak's heaven. It's a roomy, dimly-lit octagon with consoles for the control stations facing out to the respective housing units. Not only could the cell doors all be controlled from here, but also the water and lights. If someone tried to flood the pod like they did at CSP, the control center just shuts off the water. What a concept! There's an intercom to each cell that thankfully could also be turned off to quell the incessant chatter.

Three officers were always stationed in the control unit, and they scrambled like investment bankers at a congressional inquiry. Warning lights flashed and buzzers sounded, computer voices called out information or warnings. It's a zoo. All three tiers in each of the eight housing units were easily visible just by taking a lap around the octagon, each cell individually controlled from right here. It's overwhelming just to watch it, and only three of the eight units were filled so far.

A few days later we had our first "man down" at the new Centennial South. I was just arriving at the old Centennial clinic for my shift when all hell broke loose. I was in the sally port with eight officers coming on shift when master control called in and directed everyone to an emergency in the new facility. Terrible, the report said. An explosion or something. An officer and an inmate. Go! Go! Go!

So I went running with the COs across the tarmac to the rear door. And waited. We pushed the button. And waited. We could see three officers in master control through the glass. Two nurses rushed up to join us. And waited.

Finally the door slid open and we entered the core. Where was the emergency? C-Pod Level 4! We're off and running again. Wait! Two COs were running along the endless corridor coming the other way.

"Where's the emergency?" I asked the first CO.

"Nobody knows! We're trying to find them!"

"Someone said C-Pod Level 4," I said.

"We just came from there. Nobody's hurt there."

"Got a radio?"

"We've tried. Nobody knows where they are."

"What about the explosion?" I asked.

"Explosion? I didn't hear about that!"

Another CO arrived breathless. "They're on the loading dock!"

We turned and ran to the intersection at the core. I grabbed for the stair door. Locked.

"It's faster if you take the elevator," said my CO companion.

The stairwell door popped open. The nurses and I plunged down the stairs. It was only one floor. How can the elevator be faster? Locked. We wait at the bottom of the stairwell. We push the button. We wait.

Finally the door popped, and we rushed out to meet the COs who took the elevator. "Told ya, Doc. They're out there on the loading dock."

Two other nurses were finishing placing small bandages on the arms of two men, one inmate and a CO. No blood. No body parts. One cut each. Got nicked by a grinder. No explosion. I felt kind of disappointed, especially since the two other nurses had beaten us to the site just by walking across from the clinic.

This pointed out a disadvantage of working at Centennial South. It's big. Nobody knew where anybody else was, what they're doing, or what's really going on. It would likely get better with time, but I had just led the first Chinese fire drill in the big house. Maybe I could get a wall plaque.

TWENTY-NINE

GOT ANY LAST WORDS, PUNK?

The inmates I treated were felons. Juries convicted them beyond reasonable doubt of crimes of lust, greed, anger and stupidity. I rarely heard protestations of innocence. These were people
who screwed up, usually repeatedly and often big time. Especially at
Colorado State Penitentiary, the supermax, they were unrepentant and
likely to remain so.

Yet for all the horrors that brought them to my clinic, they were still
human beings with lives gone askew. It would have been easy to regard
prisoners as a separate aberrant species and the prison as a zoological
garden of queer exotics.

The inmates at CSP were different from our population of law-
abiding citizens, but to place them on a different planet would be a mistake. There was no absolute disconnect between these men and the rest
of society. Every one of us harbors a streak of dishonesty, of amorality,
of suppressed violence. Given the right circumstances we all are ca-
pable of atrocious actions.

The difference is more of a gradient rather than a gap. At one end
of the spectrum are the sociopaths of CSP who act entirely from self-
interest without empathy for others. Less extreme are those who know
what they do is wrong, but try to get by without detection. There are
those who are entangled by circumstances that make the wrong choice

appear their only option. The transition from black to white behavior allows for lots of gray.

The worst of us are still human. Even sociopaths cry in the night. Murderers miss their children. Child molesters feel fear and shame. I say this not to excuse their crimes, but to remind myself that I'm not so far removed from members of our race who didn't or couldn't do any better. It's what drives me to give my best efforts to those who others might say don't deserve it.

They might be right. Perhaps some or maybe all of these inmates don't deserve the consideration. But I didn't become a doctor so I could judge my patients or decide who deserves care. As a man I might feel differently, but the examination room is not the place for moral judgments. I'll leave that unenviable task to the courts and the clergy.

I remember rising with my fellow medical graduates at the University of Michigan, throat tight with emotion, to recite the Hippocratic Oath. It is a pledge to always act in the best interests of my patients.

Those words, centuries old, might seem nothing more than a quaint ritual to some, but like a trusted mentor I still carry every syllable into the clinic with me. As one of my patients remarked, "You really take this serious, don't you, Doc." I do. Perhaps my patient doesn't deserve the best I can offer, but for my sake I can give no less.

I'm less sanguine about working in a bureaucracy. Like the geologic process of stratification, the calcified layers that have been around the longest tend to be least adaptable and most resistant to change.

This is not a surprise. People settle in to the known and the comfortable. Change takes independent thought, courage and a little dynamite. However, high explosives are not allowed in prisons, especially in administrative offices.

The physicians, nurses, PAs, and NPs in CDOC are among the best I've ever worked with. They consistently prevail over crushing odds of budgetary privation, inadequate equipment, and draconian supervision. Stars shine in supervisory roles too, but they shine against a dark background.

I still like practicing correctional medicine, but I find myself shopping. I'm no longer willing to work with inflexible people who just want to climb the corporate ladder, and so far I've fired two bosses who had that agenda. It felt good and left me open to work with a better class of administrator.

I'm not sure how long the ride will last, but I still enjoy coming to work and believe I'm making a positive difference in some lives, including my own.

I promised my wife when I started this strange journey that I'd quit when it wasn't fun anymore. So far, so good.

Just don't turn your back on 'em.

ABOUT THE AUTHOR

William Wright, M.D., currently Medical Director of the El Paso County Criminal Justice Center, is a graduate of the University of Michigan Medical School. A private pilot, he is the holder of three black belts and instructor certifications in Tae Kwon Do and Aikido. He is a commercial artist (www.WilliamWrightArt.com) and plays guitar poorly in his spare time.

He lives in Colorado Springs with his wife, Mollie, and a variable number of fur-bearing companions. *Maximum Insecurity* is a memoir of his past eight years as the physician in Colorado's supermax prison.

ACKNOWLEDGEMENTS

The real heroes of this book are the men and women of the Colorado Department of Corrections. Unseen and underappreciated, they perform daily acts of patience, compassion, and healing to an audience of Colorado's worst criminals.

My special thanks go to the doctors, nurses, physician assistants, nurse practitioners, ward clerks, and administrators who taught me so much. Josie, Rita, Roger, Neil, Kathy, Tim, Ruby, Diane, Lynn, Mary and scores of others, you showed me that friendship and humor are just as important as penicillin.

I have to thank the prisoners as well. Not that they had much choice, but they took a suburban ear specialist and turned him into a doctor who at this point thinks he's seen damn near everything.

It would be criminally ungracious to omit thanks for the ruthless editing of Karen Lacey and Mike Sirota. If not for them, this book would have been published a year sooner to universal condemnation. Ernest Hemingway, who did not read this book, was correct in saying, "The first draft of anything is shit."

Finally to the woman who pasted, "Are you EVER coming to bed??" above my computer, I tender my eternal love and gratitude. I'll be there in just a minute.

THANK YOU

B efore you go, I'd like to say "thank you" for purchasing my book and reading it all the way to the end.

If you liked what you've read, I'd like to ask a favor.

Please take a moment to leave a review (it's painless!) on my page at Amazon.com or other retailer where you obtained the book. It really helps.

Made in the USA
Lexington, KY
12 March 2015